The Third Knife

The Third Knife

A Tale of Vengeance and Passion
in the
French Resistance

Pamela Boles Eglinski

Copyright © Pamela Boles Eglinski
September 2015
v.10.28.15

ISBN-13: 978-0692549087
ISBN-10: 0692549080

Also available in Kindle EBook

This is a work of fiction. The names, characters, and dialogue are drawn from the author's imagination. Historical events are complemented with fictitious stories and characters.

Photographer: Kruger Photography
Cover designer: Pam Kauffman
Formatting Expert: Gordon Kessler

Published by: LWF Publishing
Lawrence, KS
USA

Written by Pamela Boles Eglinski
http://www.pamelaboleseglinski.com

Endorsed by New York Times Best Selling Author

Bob Mayer

"Eglinski spins a riveting story of intrigue and sacrifice in the French Resistance. Dynamic characters and a richly layered plot encircle you at the start and refuse to let you go until the very end. For those who love historical fiction, this is an absolute 'must read'."

Bob Mayer is the author of more than 50 books, including historical novels, special ops, and non-fiction. He is a New York Times best selling author, a graduate of West Point, and a former Green Beret. I am honored to receive his endorsement.

Acknowledgments

Many thanks to the Sedulous Writers Group—my ever diligent critique group. They've helped me become the writer I am today, and they've succeeded in making my third novel, *The Third Knife,* shine brightly.

Thanks also to my manuscript proof readers: Norm Ledgin, who never ceases to "not so silently correct my grammar"; Don sloan, inveterate reader; Mary Johnson, who perfects and corrects my French, Italian, and German; and Barbara Schowen, who inevitably spots the last elusive typo.

A huge thanks goes to Pam Besler Kauffman for taking some random ideas and a couple of photos, and creating the stunning cover for *The Third Knife*.

And last in the order of things, but not least by any means, my everlasting respect goes to Gordon Kessler for his terrific job in formatting both the paperback and e-book of *The Third Knife*.

Author's Notes
Nom de Guerre (War Names)

Nearly all French Resistance fighters used false names (war names) during WWII. Each major character in *The Third Knife* assumes a *nom de guerre*. The objectives were to hide their true identity for security purposes and to protect their families from reprisal. It is a long-standing French tradition.

The characters in *The Third Knife* reclaim their real names in the final chapters of the book—transitioning the reader to the second novel in the series, *Return of the French Blue*, where many of the same personalities return.

A List of Characters is posted on the page immediately following the end of the novel. It includes the characters' real and war names.

WWII French Flags

French Tri-color | Resistance/Free French | Republic of Vercors

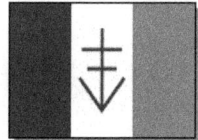

During World War II, the French flag was altered by Charles de Gaulle and by the Republic of Vercors. The French Tri-color was maintained by Vichy France (originally unoccupied), which was governed by Marshal Petain.

Both de Gaulle and the Resistance movement felt Petain "sold out" to the Germans. In response, they created an alternate flag – one embraced by the Free French Army, the Resistance movement in the large cities, and the French *Maquis*. The Cross of Lorraine, centered on the white, was emblematic of Joan of Arc, patron saint of France, and was used by de Gaulle as a symbolic response to the ubiquitous swastika.

The flag of the Republic of Vercors was created when the province declared independence from both France and Germany. The "V" at the base of the cross symbolizes Vercors, and victory.

The Resistance flag is emblematic of French determination, resilience, and ultimate victory over the brutality unleashed on them by the German army and Gestapo during the occupation.

Chapter 1
Settevendemie Farmhouse
Torino, Italy, October 1943

Darkness settled in and a cold rain fell. The wind caught Catalina's long wool skirt, whipping it around her legs, causing her to stumble.

Someone grasped her arm and removed the pail of milk from her shaking hands. "Let me help, Catalina. It's bitter cold, and you should be inside."

"Lorenzo!" Her breath caught. "You frightened me. My father will be angry if he knows you're here."

"Angry because I've joined the German army? The Germans are our allies."

"*Were* our allies," she said. "The Americans have landed in Sicily, and Mussolini is in prison. Italy has joined the Allies."

"Don't be foolish. We'll fight alongside the Germans. And tell your father to keep his opinions to himself. It's dangerous not to side with the Germans."

"My brother will be home soon," Catalina said,

stiffening her back. "He'll protect us, and Father has a gun."

"Pietro won't come home. He deserted the army. If he's found, he'll be shot," Lorenzo said.

"You're a liar!" Catalina spat. "Pietro wouldn't abandon his country. He's not like you."

The back door swung open. Adelle, Catalina's mother, took a step forward, peering into the darkness. "Are you finished with the chores, Catalina? It's cold and wet outside. Come in."

"I'm on my way. The cows gave a lot of milk. The pail is heavy."

She reached for the handle and whispered, "Leave, Lorenzo. Your chance to court me is over. Go back to your German friends—the *Boches*."

"I'll leave, but I'm telling you—don't speak ill of our allies."

"*Buona notte*, Lorenzo," Catalina hissed, turning her back on him and stepping into the farmhouse.

"You're shivering," Adelle said. "Give me the milk, and go stand by the fire. I've baked bread, and the stew is nearly ready."

Catalina removed her beret. Her long ebony hair tumbled past her shoulders. "The stew smells wonderful," she said, shrugging out of her coat. "We don't often have meat. Is this a special occasion?"

"Give me your coat," said her father. "I'll hang it by the fire to dry."

"Father, I'm worried. The Germans are advancing from the north, and the Allies have landed in Sicily. I've seen pictures of the Great War. Trees stripped of leaves and branches. Farmland burned and turned under. Will it happen here?"

"You think too much," Nico said. "Let's eat. Then I'll share the news." They sat, joined hands, and said a prayer for their country and Pietro.

When spoons scraped the bottom of the bowls and fresh bread sopped the last of the gravy, Nico moved his chair back from the table, crossed his legs, and took a deep breath.

"Catalina, you must leave Italy. Tonight. A guide is coming. He'll take you to France."

"Tonight? Why? You and Mother need me!"

"It's too dangerous for you to stay here," he said. "Since Italy surrendered to the Allies, the German army has moved into the north. I've heard terrible stories about how they treat women, especially the young and beautiful ones, like you." He shook his head.

"Don't frighten me, Father. I can't leave you. You know that. I won't yield to the Germans and run. And what about Pietro. He'll need our help."

"We'll take care of each other," Nico said. "You'll be safer in Nice, with your aunt Francine. She'll take you in, shelter you until the war is over."

"*Zia* Francine hasn't spoken to us in years. You know that. Mother's family hates Italians. They're still angry at her for marrying you. War or not, they won't welcome me."

Nico shook his head. "She'll come around."

"And if she doesn't? Then what? The Germans

occupy *all* of France. Where will I go? Return to Torino as the Germans advance south? If you fear for my safety now—*that* would be the time."

"If Francine won't accept you, then you'll need to search for our old friends, the Bonhommes. They live in the Russian quarter. Remember their son, Edouard? The two of you used to play on the beach, searching for sand-washed stones. You'd set up a little stand on the Promenade," he said wistfully, "where you sold them to the tourists for *centimes*."

"Father, I don't understand. *Please* let me stay. We're family. I can't abandon you and Mother."

"There is another reason you need to leave," Nico said.

"What could be more important than our lives?" she asked angrily.

"The blue diamond necklace. It must be hidden. It's been in the family since the French Revolution. The Germans know about it, and will come looking. Our family fortune will be lost. You need to carry the necklace with you. Safeguard it."

Adelle pulled a strand of diamonds, which she'd wrapped in fabric, from the jar above the sink. She tied it around Catalina's waist.

Stepping back to admire her work she said, "Now the stones are safe, and you will be, too. The French Blues have always brought us luck. When the war is over, you'll bring them back, and we'll rebuild our vineyards."

Catalina adjusted her new "belt," fluffing her

blouse out to cover the muslin-wrapped diamonds.

A knock sounded at the door. "It must be Rafael," Nico said. "He's your guide. He'll take you to your aunt's home, in Nice."

"I need time to say good-bye, to you and our friends. Don't make me slink off in the night," Catalina pleaded.

Adelle took Catalina in her arms and held her close. Nico hugged them both and whispered. "Come back when the war is over. Pietro will return, too. Now go, Rafael is waiting."

Chapter 2
Carignano, Italy
Next Morning

Rafael, a short muscular man with dark bushy eyebrows and a wool beret perched to the side of his head, led the way.

"The sun is rising," Catalina said. "We've walked all night. Can't we rest?"

"Two more kilometers, *signorina*. We'll spend the day in an abbey. Eat and sleep. Then walk again at night."

"You know the trail well," Catalina said.

"I've led many Italians to safety."

"Look," she said, pointing across the meadow. "A village—over there, through the mist."

"Move quietly," Rafael whispered. "We'll head down the hill, then turn to the left. Look for the abbey."

They hunched over, making their way through tall wet grass.

"Come here," a man said, appearing out of the mist.

"Through the side door. Quickly."

"The monk is our contact," Rafael whispered.

Catalina slipped through the door, followed by Rafael and their host, a man in a brown hooded robe. He held his finger to his lips, as though every word could be heard by the Führer in Berlin. He led them toward a side-aisle with a small door on an interior wall. The monk unlocked it carefully, turning the key without a sound, ushering them down the steps into the necropolis.

A single candle burned in a dish near the tombs. The dark room smelled of rat droppings and rotten flowers. Dripping water echoed through the underground chamber. Each step yielded the crunch of dried insects and dead spiders.

The monk motioned them to follow. On the far side of the room, he stopped, felt for a loose stone in the wall, and wriggled it free. Reaching through, he pulled a chain on the opposite side. A hidden door popped open.

"I've prepared the room for you," the monk said.

Beyond the door, two candles burned in a tiny room. Blankets were folded and stacked against the far wall.

"You'll be safe here. This tomb is for the living." The monk spoke softly. "It's good to see you, Rafael. You bring a woman this time."

"Yes, but the less you know the better."

"I understand." The monk bowed his head. "There is food on the table," he gestured, "and wine to wash it down. Use the blankets under and over you, or the stones will exchange their icy cold for your warmth."

Catalina nodded as the two men shook hands.

"Extinguish the candles before you sleep. You can use the large flashlight under the table when you wake." With a click of the door and the scrape of stone, he was gone.

"*Signorina*," Rafael said. "Put your coat over here, where it can dry, then wrap yourself in blankets, eat, and sleep. In the afternoon, I'll show you our map and give you your forged papers, a new name, and some money.

***

Catalina opened her eyes slowly, rubbing away the blurriness that comes with too little sleep. Rafael sat at the small table, a map spread before him. The glow of a single candle illuminated the room with a flickering light.

"*Signorina*," Rafael said. "Come study the map."

Catalina moved to the table, clutching a blanket around her shoulders.

"The trail runs south from Torino to Mondovi," Rafael said, moving his finger along the map. "From Mondovi, we head southeast toward the Mediterranean. When we reach Savona, we turn west and hike along the coast to the French border. Altogether it's two hundred kilometers."

"It's not a direct route," Catalina said. "We head east and then west. Why?"

"This is the easiest path. It winds through the green valleys that lead to the coast. It's longer, but we make better time than walking directly south to the coast. That trail," he pointed at the map, "would take us through the Maritime Alps, where the weather is much more severe and unpredictable. *Capisci?*"

"Is the trail well marked?" Catalina asked.

"Cairns guide us, but it's well used. If something should happen to me, you won't have trouble finding your way."

Catalina nodded, wondering what could possibly happen.

"We'll walk along the Po River tonight," he said. Catalina bent closer to follow his finger on the map. "The path is next to the river. It's not a difficult walk, and the flowing water masks our footsteps. If needed, we can hide in boulders along the way. We'll have some moonlight, and I know the trail well. We'll make good time."

"A lot of details," Catalina murmured.

"When the monk returns, we'll ask what he knows about German military encampments. Now, take these papers. They're your new identity. Your *nom de guerre* is Charlotte Beaumont. I'll call you Charlotte from now on. Push these papers deep into your pocket, and *do not* lose them."

Catalina swallowed. This was more frightening than she'd imagined.

"Also, we'll pose as a couple," Rafael said. "We draw less attention that way."

"In Torino I heard that the Germans were moving south, toward Rome," Catalina said.

Rafael nodded. "I heard the same. Now get your coat and your shoes. Our host will arrive soon. If you have some coins, give him a few. His work is dangerous."

The door to the chamber rattled, and the monk stepped in.

Chapter 3
Carmagnola, Italy

The distant mountains were aglow with the rising sun—a welcome sight after walking all night. Charlotte heaved a sigh of relief. She was not used to so much walking. Her shoes were old, and blisters were forming.

Rafael pointed to large boulders above the trail. "We'll sleep among the stones today. There's a little nest of straw between several boulders. It's a resting place, known to guides like myself."

A hint of early light crept across the nearby fields. Charlotte watched Rafael as he scanned the area for movement. "Follow me," he said, satisfied.

Exhausted, Charlotte paid little attention to where she placed her feet. Rafael reached out to help her over the last boulder, but the rock shifted. She teetered, and slipped—her leg wedged between two large stones.

"Charlotte!"

"My leg," she cried. "I'm trapped."

"Shuu." He tried to calm her. "We'll work together.

When we move the rock, quickly pull your leg free."

Charlotte groaned, twisting just enough to gain some leverage.

"I'll count to three. You push, I'll pull," Rafael said.

The large stone moved, but not enough.

"Push again!"

Finally, Charlotte pulled her leg free.

"Can you put weight on it?" he asked.

"I … I think so."

He supported her as they stepped down into the hideout.

She sat with her back against a boulder and surveyed the damage.

"You scraped your head, too. There's a little blood," Rafael said, a worried frown on his face. "How does your leg feel?"

Pulling her skirt up to her knee, she massaged her calf. "I feel a lump, but it's not broken, just some scrapes. I can wiggle my toes," she said, smiling.

Rafael rummaged in his pack. "I have alcohol and bandages. This will sting. *Don't* cry out." He looked at her head next. Wiping it clean, he said, "You're bruised, but neither wound is serious."

Charlotte gritted her teeth against the pain and nodded her thanks.

"Be careful," he said. "We have a lot of walking to do. You'll need your feet and your head. Now, pocket the rag. We leave nothing behind."

***

She awoke with a start. Rafael was gone! Men were arguing down on the trail, a few meters away. Germans. She recognized the guttural tones, understanding most of what they said.

"There is no time to spare," the German said. "We must be in Savona in three days—then march to Rome." The soldier sounded like he was in charge.

She heard more conversation from the river, and the splashing of men filling their canteens.

Then the commander's voice again. "Finish eating and drinking. We're moving out—now!"

She waited a few minutes before peeking over the boulders. The path was clear. She saw Rafael across the Po. He crawled through the grass. When he reached the river, he jumped from stone to stone—crossing easily. Within minutes he was at her side.

"That was close," whispered Rafael, as he dropped down among the boulders. "German troops everywhere. We're on the same path. Trucks and heavy machinery are on the road just above us. I saw them across the river."

"They were talking about marching to Rome," Charlotte said. "But, Rafael, please don't ever leave without waking me first. I thought you'd abandoned me."

"I'm sorry *signorina*. You were sleeping so soundly. I bought food in the market."

She sighed deeply, and thanked him. Her father said to trust him. Surely he was right.

***

Late in the afternoon, Charlotte heard German voices again. She shook Rafael. His eyes opened wide. She held a finger to her lips. This time the voices came from the road.

As the soldiers moved away, Rafael unfolded his map and spread it on the ground. In a low voice, he said, "We need to change our plans. We can't go to Savona, not with the German army marching to the coast on the same trail. At Racconigi the path divides."

He pointed to the map. "We'll take the western trail, even though it's more difficult. It skirts the Alps, then drops down to Menton and the French border. There could be snow and very cold nights, but there's no choice."

Charlotte traced the route with her finger, memorizing the towns along the way. South to the sea, then west to Nice. She hoped the cairns would be easy to find.

"We should reach Racconigi in the morning," Rafael continued. "I know a safe house. We'll go there first, then find the local market. Buy food and blankets. Once we leave Racconigi, we'll be fortunate to sleep in barns and deserted homes. It'll be cold."

Chapter 4
Maritime Alps
Racconigi, Italy

When darkness settled, they moved on, stopping only to listen for sounds of other travelers, and soldiers approaching.

"Are you alright?" Rafael asked. "How's your leg?"

"Sore, but I can keep up."

"Shh! I hear someone. Hide," he said, pulling Charlotte down behind some bushes.

"Who were they?" she whispered after the men passed.

"Italians. Military. Maybe deserters, maybe not. Perhaps they're headed south to link up with the Germans. We can't trust anyone."

They reached Racconigi just as sun flooded the tiny village square. The safe house was easy to find, but no one answered the door when Rafael knocked. He frowned at Charlotte, concern in his eyes. The sun had risen. They needed a place to hide. Soon.

Rafael tried the latch. It lifted. Pushing against the door, he entered and examined the room. The windows were open. A thick layer of dust covered the floor. Fresh footprints signaled recent visitors.

Rafael motioned for Charlotte to follow. Closing the door behind them, they searched every room upstairs and down.

"Can we stay here?" Charlotte asked.

"No. The family may have been exposed—shipped off somewhere or killed. The Germans could have left the door open to trap people like you and me, seeking refuge."

The front door creaked. Rafael held a finger to his lips, pushing Charlotte into the pantry. He slipped in behind her and closed the door. She held her breath and listened as someone walked through the house.

"We left footprints," she whispered.

Rafael groaned, and reached into his boot for a dagger. Charlotte stepped back. The crunch of dried pasta underfoot echoed like a shot in the empty house. She gasped, pressing her palm over her mouth.

The pantry door swung open. A young German soldier pointed his rifle at them. His hands shook.

Rafael knocked the gun aside and thrust the dagger into the soldier's chest.

The boy's eyes glazed. He fell. Dead within seconds.

Charlotte gasped, squeezed her eyes shut, and choked back vomit.

Rafael grabbed her wrist and pulled her out of the room. "We need to hide. The Germans will come looking for him, then search for the killer."

They stumbled out the front door and slipped into a nearby alley. Catching his breath, Rafael said, "I know a priest. His church is across town. It's Sunday morning. Families will be on their way to Mass. Let's walk with them."

Approaching the church, they stepped into the shade of a nearby tree. Rafael lit a cigarette.

"Sit, here, on the bench," said Rafael. "And don't look worried. When the priest enters the side door, we'll follow him in."

Charlotte glanced at Rafael. Though he tried to act nonchalant, his hand shook. He'd just killed a man. And now, they may be hunted.

***

"I hope no one saw you leave the safe house," the priest said, pressing a baguette into their hands. "It's all I can spare. Now, take this water." He handed them a pitcher. "Clean yourselves up. There is still blood on your hands. I'll return late in the afternoon. Do *not* leave this room."

Charlotte and Rafael tried to sleep, but with little success. Late in the afternoon, she heard a key in the lock.

The priest entered. "Germans are everywhere. Guards watch every road and path leaving town. They suspect a man and a woman. Someone must have seen you leave the house. I'll help you get out of the village.

Here is a little more food for today and tomorrow. I've brought blankets, too." The priest handed them a bundle.

"This is how you'll escape," the priest said. "A large conduit carries spring snowmelt from the forest into the village cisterns. It's dry now, and you can walk through it. It's nearly two kilometers long, and you'll have to crouch as you work your way through. It exits in a gully, slightly west of the trail."

"Do the Germans know about the conduit?" Rafael asked.

The priest shook his head. "I don't think so. It empties directly into the cisterns, about three meters below ground level. The water is four meters deep. If you fall in, you'll drown."

Rafael nodded. It was risky, and wouldn't be easy. But they had no choice.

"Don't light a candle until you're well into the pipe. I'll give you four candles. Burn one at a time. They should last the entire distance."

The priest handed Rafael a cloth bag. "Put everything in here and tie it around your waist. Your hands need to be free. I'll meet you at midnight. Be ready to go."

***

"*Signorina*," the priest whispered, "stand back against the wall." The men bent to move the cistern cover. A grinding of metal against metal filled the air. "Get down! In the shadows," the priest hissed, "and pray the Nazis didn't hear."

They waited a minute, then crept back to the cistern. Rafael laced the rope under his arms, wound the end of the rope over the main rope, and slipped into the hole. The priest helped Charlotte next. Rafael caught her legs and pulled her inside the conduit. Then he let the rope slip away. It slithered up the shaft and out of sight. The priest pushed the cover back in place.

Rafael took Charlotte by the hand. Crouching and scrambling in the dark, they moved forward. Something scurried past Charlotte, brushing her leg. She gasped, stifling a scream.

"What's the matter?" asked Rafael.

"Maybe a rat. Don't know. It stinks down here." She shuddered.

"Stay close," whispered Rafael. "Don't talk unless you have to. Our voices echo."

The air in the pipe was warmer than above ground, but that was little comfort. Their backs ached as they hobbled through the tube, hunched to avoid hitting their heads. Rafael insisted they stop often to listen for sounds within the pipe and above. They felt the vibrations of a truck, but nothing more.

Nearing the end of the tunnel they saw a glimmer of light, just as their last candle sputtered out.

Rafael whispered, "Stay here." He moved toward the exit, then suddenly halted.

Charlotte's breathing echoed in the silence. Then ... the sound of voices. Italian voices. Up above. A group of men? She squatted, listening.

"A German was knifed yesterday," an Italian said.

"The *Boches* will think we did it. We need to get to the coast. More places to hide, and it'll be warmer. No more ice and snow."

Another man voiced support. "We can find safety in Menton. Many Italians live there—and they're *not* German sympathizers."

"Let's go. It's too cold and dangerous to stand here talking." That last voice sounded like Pietro. Could it be …? She wondered.

Light disappeared as the campfire died out. Once again darkness surrounded Rafael and Charlotte.

They waited a few moments then felt their way to the end of the conduit. A crude wooden lattice, covered with dried leaves and brush, marked the exit.

Rafael pushed the cover up an inch at a time peering through the opening. The moon sent a shaft of light into the pipe. "They're gone," he announced, moving the cover aside. He scrambled out, pulling Charlotte up after him. An eerie quiet and bitter cold surrounded them. They'd have to move quickly—both to stay warm and to put distance between them and any Germans that might follow.

Chapter 5
Savigliano, Italy
Maritime Alps
East of Grenoble

The piney smell of dry larch needles filled the air. Dead leaves crackled underfoot and swirling winds blew through the valley, bringing dark gray clouds and frigid air. The rock-strewn trail grew narrow and steep. Patches of snow and ice covered the trail. Ibex and chamois, rarely seen at lower altitudes, fed on wild grasses in the woods.

The icy wind brought an ominous solitude, even though Rafael walked only a few steps ahead.

"The Italians are probably on the run, just ahead of us," Rafael said. "And the Germans—behind."

"Need to catch my breath," Charlotte said, leaning against a tree.

"*Merda!*" Rafael swore, holding out his hand. "Snow. Makes walking even more difficult. It's too cold to hide in the woods until nightfall. We'll have to walk during the day—and reach Savigliano before dark. Come."

Charlotte took a deep breath before she pushed herself upright. Pressing her shoulders back, she followed the seemingly tireless Rafael.

They'd nearly reached the village when Rafael stopped abruptly. "Quiet! I hear someone. Get over here."

Charlotte heard Germans speaking. "Are we looking for Italian deserters?" a soldier asked, "or a man and a woman?"

"Both," another voice said. Germans in uniform came into view. One spit on the ground. "We'll find them. And when we do...."

A soldier pointed to a nearby pasture. "There's a barn. Maybe they're hiding inside." The soldiers ran toward the building, surrounded it and rushed inside. The search resulted in flushing out a small goat. The Germans left—moving on down the trail.

"The *Boches* may stop to eat. We don't want to overtake them," whispered Rafael. The snow made walking more treacherous. Charlotte blew on her hands, trying to warm them.

Then, the sound of automatic gunfire and screams filled the mountain air. Gruesome sounds echoed through the valley. Charlotte slipped and fell to her knees.

Rafael pulled her off the trail—pushing her behind trees.

He retrieved his pistol and removed the safety.

She held her breath.

The German voices grew less distinct—they were moving away, down the trail.

Dieu merci.

When sounds from the German troops faded, the couple returned to the trail. Rounding the bend they immediately saw the slaughtered men. Twisted bodies lay across the path. Blood turned the white snow crimson. Dead eyes stared upwards—toward the heavens.

One face caught Charlotte in a flash of recognition. Pietro. She *had* heard him on the trail earlier. Staggering toward her brother's contorted body, she fell to her knees.

"Please, God. Not my brother." She bent over his body, shaking him, trying to bring him back to life. Rafael pressed his hand over her mouth before she screamed. "Charlotte," he said, "I'm so sorry. They are all dead. We can't stay. The Germans might double back."

She wiped Pietro's bloody face with her handerchief, then drew a cross on his forehead with her thumb. *"Dio benedica la tua anima.* May God bless your soul."

"Mourn later," Rafael said. "Let me check your brother's pockets. We'll take any mementos."

The dog tags were gone. A trophy for the Nazis. "A St-Anne medal and a dagger," Rafael said, handing them to her. "Take these. Now go. "

Charlotte stood, swayed, and nearly fell. Rafael

caught her. She focused on the crimson snow. "So much blood," she whispered, tucking the knife in her pocket and fastening the gold medal around her neck. "St-Anne—the protector of women and children." She spoke to Pietro. "A gift from Mother when you went to war."

They staggered down the path.

"There is an abandoned abbey just ahead. Follow me." Rafael led Charlotte to a small room on the side of the chapel.

Exhausted, they spread their blankets and lay down.

Charlotte whispered to the darkness. "Pietro was my best friend. He was to inherit the vineyard—carry on the family name. Now," she choked, "it'll never happen."

"The war will change our country forever. Survivors will grieve for a lifetime." Rafael paused. "Try to sleep. Tomorrow comes too soon."

Chapter 6
Cuneo, Italy
Maritime Alps
Two Days Later

Cuneo, once a charming village tucked into a lush valley, was weathered and bleak. Rusted metal gates hung at odd angles, desperate for paint and repair. Houses covered with soot, outer walls crumbling, cried out for care. Trash filled the streets. Pride of home and country—abandoned. Snow covered the piazza. The once popular market was nearly empty.

Charlotte waited on a side street, in a small alcove. Pietro's dead face haunted her.

The sound of heavy boots approached. Pulling back into the shadows, she sat on the cobbles, drew her knees to her chin, and stared at the ground. The boots came to an abrupt stop in front of her.

"Papers, *bitte*," demanded the Nazi. "And stand when I address you! Get up! Get up!"

"*Naturalmente*," Charlotte replied, taking her time.

"*Mach schnell!* I can't wait all day for you slow-witted Italians."

"Here." She coughed on her identification papers as she handed them over. Groaning, she reached into her pocket for the rag stained with Pietro's blood. She coughed again, spitting into the cloth.

"Are you coughing blood? Do you have tuberculosis?"

"A bad cold. From winters without heat. Many villagers are sick."

"Take your papers and get away from me. You Italians are weak. The world would be better without you, like the Jews. Go! If I discover you have TB, I'll put you on the next train to Ravensbrück."

Charlotte hurried away then circled back to the market where she found Rafael. "The Germans are patrolling Cuneo," she said. "One just stopped me. Give me something to carry, so we look like a couple shopping."

"The path to Limone Piemonte is just ahead," Rafael said, handing her some packages. "We'll move down that street," he gestured. "Then into the forest, about a hundred meters south. From there, onto the trail."

"You seem anxious," said Charlotte. "What's wrong?"

"I'll tell you later. Follow me and say nothing."

Within five minutes, they were in a neighborhood of small stone bungalows with slate-gray roofs and tiny garden plots blanketed with snow.

"We'll slip between the houses and across the field."

A woman peered at them, over café curtains. "Rafael, we're being watched."

"I know. I saw her, too. Walk quickly, but don't run. We'll be among the trees soon."

He looked back as they entered a copse of leafless poplars. No one followed, but their footprints remained in the snow.

"Tuck the food into your coat pockets," Rafael said. "So your hands are free. You can move more easily that way."

"Alright, but what happened back there?" Charlotte persisted.

"I saw someone I know," he said.

"Who?" Charlotte paused to look at Rafael.

"Keep moving," he said. "You've never asked why I guide people from Italy to France and Switzerland."

"I assumed you had your reasons," Charlotte said.

"Mussolini ordered my father killed. Il Duce had him hanged in a public square. His crime? Publishing pamphlets against fascism. My mother was raped until she died." Rafael choked on his words. "By a gang of fascists. I saw both my parents murdered."

"*Dio*," she whispered, holding her hand to her mouth.

"One night soldiers came for me. They said if I didn't join the army they'd kill me. I went, but within weeks I deserted and began helping others escape."

"A dangerous choice. Weren't you afraid?" she

asked.

"Yes, but I couldn't stay with those murderers. Now, the Gestapo has a price on my head," Rafael continued. "One dedicated assassin has made it his mission to find and kill me. I saw him in the market. He may have seen me, too."

"Maybe we should go back to our old pattern. Camp during the day and walk at night," Charlotte said.

"No. He might get ahead of us, realize his mistake, and lie in wait. I'd rather try to outrun him. If he comes from behind, I want to be between you and him."

***

"We need to catch our breath, stop and eat," Rafael said. "A ravine runs parallel to the trail, just below. We should be safe down there. Follow."

A rifle shot echoed across the valley floor. Rafael clutched his chest and fell to the ground.

Charlotte's eyes flashed from Rafael to the Nazi moving toward her. The German's finger twitched on the trigger of his rifle, its barrel pointed toward the ground.

My mother was raped until she died ... Charlotte stepped back. The soldier matched her step for step. She stumbled over a tree root, but caught herself. He tried to grab her. She leapt away.

Another shot. The Nazi grabbed his shoulder, blood running through his fingers.

"Rafael!"

Despite his wound, the Nazi fired again at Rafael. But his shot went high. Charlotte had grabbed the

German's head, pulled it back, and slashed his throat. Pietro's knife found vengeance.

The soldier toppled to the ground, blood gurgling from his mouth.

She ran to Rafael, knelt, and pressed his hand to her cheek. "Please, please don't leave me," she choked.

A weak smile crossed his lips. He reached toward her face, but life slipped away before he could touch her. "*Addio,*" she said, bending over him, sobbing.

A twig snapped in the brush.

Charlotte jerked, touching the St-Anne medal at her throat. "Who's there?"

A large hairy ibex with massive scimitar-shaped horns stepped onto the path, locking eyes with her.

Her breath caught. The animal turned and walked down the slope into the ravine.

She gasped for air, her heart still pounding. With shaking hands Charlotte reached inside Rafael's jacket. She removed his identification papers and the map, then pocketed his pistol.

Bending over one more time she whispered, "Good-bye, my friend. *Che Dio ti benedica.* We will win this war, I promise you."

She kissed his forehead, touched his cheek, turned, and ran.

Chapter 7
Near Menton, France

The morning sun flickered across the mountaintops as Charlotte approached a small farmhouse. She'd walked for three nights, sleeping in the woods during the day. Hunger and exhaustion overwhelmed caution as she sought refuge in the nearby barn.

Chickens scattered as she stumbled through an open door. A cow stirred in its stall and a rooster crowed. She lurched toward a ladder propped against the loft. Grasping for one of the rungs, she missed and fell to the floor.

***

"*Signorina*. Wake up," said the farmer. "You can't stay here. It's too cold. There's food in the house and a fire. Let me help you."

He pulled Charlotte upright, put his arm around her waist, and walked her to the kitchen.

"Sit," he said, as they entered the room. "The chair is old but comfortable."

Charlotte sank into the armchair. Taking a deep breath, she laid her head back, exhausted but not quite asleep.

"The Germans check the houses routinely," the farmer whispered to his wife. "We must be careful."

"But she needs to eat and rest. There is coffee and polenta. I'll fry some eggs."

The man brought Charlotte a mug. "*Signorina,* drink some coffee, it will warm you."

"*Grazie.* My hands are shaking. I haven't eaten in days," Charlotte said, cupping her hands around the warm mug. "I'm so cold. *Molto grazie.* I'm surprised the Germans haven't found me."

"Here. Eat some polenta and eggs," the wife said.

"You're very kind, but you put yourselves in great danger. Why?" Charlotte asked, taking a bite.

"We are patriots of both Italy and France," the farmer answered, rubbing his hands by the fire. "May I ask where you are from, *Signorina?*"

"The less you know the better. I'm going to France. That's all I should say."

The wife nodded. "Now rest. Come. We have a room where you can sleep. You're near Menton. You can walk there tonight."

***

Charlotte woke with a start. Voices came from the kitchen, first raised and then hushed. She heard the couple and another man, talking. She crept to the closed door and listened. The voice was familiar.

There was a knock at the door. She leapt back,

groping for Pietro's knife. The door opened. "Catalina, I am here to help you," Lorenzo said. She'd seen him last in Torino, the night she left home.

Her voice shook. "Are you planning to turn me over to the Gestapo?"

"Come," Lorenzo said. "We can talk in the kitchen."

As they sat, Charlotte frowned at her hosts. Was there no one she could trust?

"You were right," Lorenzo confessed. "The Germans are *not* our allies."

She pulled Pietro's knife from her sleeve and placed it on the table. "This is my brother's dagger. The Germans killed him."

Lorenzo closed his eyes and hung his head. "Yes, I heard. I thought you'd be on the same trail, and asked a few friends to watch for you."

"Why?" asked Charlotte. "You're a German collaborator."

"You're linked with killing two Germans, one a highly trained assassin," Lorenzo said. "The Gestapo wants your head. They've circulated a flyer, including a clumsy sketch of your face. You're in great danger."

"But Lorenzo...."

"Let me finish. They've talked to your aunt, bullied her into turning you over if you show up at her house. And they've threatened your uncle."

"*Mon Dieu*." She whispered.

"You must hide. Stay away from the Germans until the war is over or. . . ."

"Or what?" Charlotte asked.

"Join the French Resistance—the *Maquis*. They fight in the countryside, outside the big cities. They work in small groups, cells, throughout France. I remember you speaking of a childhood friend, Edouard Bonhomme. Some say he leads one of these cells. But the *Maquis* are hard to find. It won't be easy to connect."

"If the Gestapo can't find them, how can I?" Charlotte asked.

"I'll explain. First, you need to get to France. You can't walk the main roads. It's too dangerous. They're clogged with trucks, German soldiers, and tanks."

"There's a bus for civilians that goes to Nice. It leaves Menton every morning at 5h00. Most of the route is on a narrow road alongside the sea. Very few Germans use it."

"Lorenzo, you put yourself in terrible danger by helping me."

"Don't worry about me," he said.

"I don't understand. Tell me why you've changed your mind. A few weeks ago you embraced the Germans."

Lorenzo drew in a sharp breath. "This is my reason. As part of my training in 'the German way' I was taken to a Gestapo prison. I was forced to watch our men, Italians, being tortured. I wanted to desert, like Pietro. I'd heard of some Resistance fighters in Menton. I met with them. They suggested I remain with the German army—gather information and help those who were in danger or trying to escape." He cleared his throat. "This brings me to you."

Charlotte touched Lorenzo's arm. "You could be caught and tortured, just like the others."

He shook his head. "I'm willing to take the chance. It's the least I can do for Pietro and your family.

"Now, listen carefully. To get on the bus in Menton you'll need a signed pass. I have one for you. Present it with your ID papers as you board. You do have papers in another name, *si?*"

"Of course."

"You'll also need to disguise yourself. The Gestapo sketch has your hair pulled back. You're wearing a beret, and a patterned shirt." He turned to the farmer's wife. "Can you give her one of your shirts?"

The woman nodded.

Lorenzo slipped her some *lire,* then told Charlotte, "With your hair down, a scarf, and a different shirt, you should make it through without a problem. Avoid eye contact, and don't look or act anxious."

Charlotte sighed. Exhaustion laced with fear.

"There are a few more things you need to remember. First, catch the bus near Chappelle St-Jacques, north of the beach on the east side of the city. It is not difficult to find. There are thirty seats, and people will be waiting. Board the bus with them."

"I remember the station," Charlotte said.

"Get off before reaching Nice. Villefranche or Beaulieu. Stay away from the Nice bus station. The Gestapo routinely patrol. Find an inexpensive hotel in the old part of Nice. Eat in cafés frequented by foreigners and patriots. I'll give you a list. If you're lucky, someone will approach you. This is when you are most vulnerable—to trust them or not. Be *very* careful. The right person can connect you with the Resistance, the wrong one to the Gestapo. Some French turn on their own countrymen. Collaborators."

She nodded, worrying already about whom to trust.

"Your hosts will hide you the rest of the day. Walk at night. I'll be watching for you tomorrow morning, near the bus terminal. I want to be certain you're safe."

"*Grazie*, Lorenzo."

He stood and took Charlotte's hand. "We will meet again when the war is over."

Chapter 8
Le Vieux Nice
Old Nice

The hotel was small and inexpensive, but it was the best she'd seen since leaving home. She bathed and ate, then washed a few clothes. Allowing herself a short nap, Charlotte lay down.

Twelve hours later she awoke to a room filled with drifting shadows. The street lamp just beyond her window gave off a dull glow. She pulled the curtain back and peered out. The city was deathly quiet. Wartime curfew.

In the morning, light washed the gloominess from the streets. Tiny shops, narrow alleys, and small cafés defined Old Nice. The square just outside St-Jacques chapel was a popular meeting place even in wartime. Charlotte selected a restaurant with a sign that promised excellent *"Croissants et Café."*

She took a table in the middle of the room. People came and went, but no one approached her. She visited several more cafés, where she overheard someone mention the Falicon *Maquis*. If she could find the cell, they might be able to lead her to Edouard.

As the sun set, she tried one more possibility— Place de Garibaldi, the northern edge of Nice, on the way to Falicon.

Perhaps, she reasoned, the *Maquis* will approach me here, on the edge of town, away from threatening eyes.

She spotted an empty bench and sat down.

Within minutes, a tall young man joined her. "Who are you?" he asked, his hand to his mouth and eyes cast down. "Are you looking for someone?" His dialect was the same as her mother's—Provençal French.

"I'm searching for a friend," she said.

"His name?"

"Edouard. *Un bon homme,*" she said.

"What do you think the good man can do for you?" the stranger asked.

"I seek vengeance. Edouard Bonhomme is an old friend. I hear he joined the Resistance. I want to help. I'm fluent in French and Italian, and know some German." She paused. "And I know how to use a dagger."

The man bit his lower lip. "Return at midnight. A friend will meet you over there," he nodded toward an alley between two buildings. "Be prepared to walk."

He was gone as quickly as he came.

***

Long after midnight, Charlotte waited alone in the

alley. She was about to return to the hotel, when a man appeared and motioned her to follow him. "Don't talk," he warned.

In the moonlight she read a street sign marked Gorges du Gabre, and Falicon. The walk was easy until they reached a grove of poplars, then the road wound steeply upward and away from Nice. Twenty minutes later she noticed a light flashing up ahead. Two flashes, a pause, then two more. Her companion responded with a flashlight—three quick bursts of light.

Charlotte exhaled slowly. The Gestapo wouldn't play these secretive games. They'd just pull me off the street, take me in for questioning, and then—torture. No. I've found the *Maquis,* and I pray Edouard Bonhomme is among them.

Chapter 9
The French Maquis
Village of Falicon

Edouard stood outside the *Maquis* hideout—a farmhouse nestled among the trees on the edge of the village. He smoked a cigarette and waited. His small band of *maquisards* worked the French Riviera gathering information on German troop movements and the Gestapo. They'd seen flyers of Catalina Settevendemie, posted around Nice.

He recognized his childhood friend. Long dark hair, high cheeks, and fair skin. Ten years had passed and the world changed. But why did she risk coming to Nice, and what did she want from the *Maquis*?

***

Two men stepped from the shadows as Catalina neared the center of the village. She shuddered, frightened, but followed them.

No one spoke. One man blindfolded her with a scarf that smelled of sweat and smoke. He tightened it at the back of her head. A solid knot.

They led her beyond the village, among the rustling trees. The air felt cold and damp against her skin. Guided by the men, she stumbled along a rock-strewn path.

She stopped and pulled back. "Where are you taking me?"

"Don't talk," a man replied, grabbing her hand and pulling her along.

The wind picked up and a chill ran through her. Her breath came in short gasps. They walked on—about 200 paces.

A light penetrated her blindfold. Not far away. She smelled kerosene. Guiding her toward the lantern, the men came to a sudden stop.

"Take off the blindfold," someone said.

She blinked as the man in front of her came into focus. He resembled her childhood friend. Tall and slim, with black hair that curled about his neck, and a gentle smile. Now, in his early twenties.

"Edouard," Catalina said, "it *is* you." A tear ran down her cheek, but she quickly brushed it away.

He moved toward her, taking her hands in his. "You're cold. We have a small fire inside. Follow me."

As they entered the house, a young man stepped forward and helped Catalina with her coat, hanging it on a nail by the door.

"Take this," a woman said, handing her a cup. "The tea is weak. We use the leaves many times, but it will warm you."

"This is Marie," Edouard said, motioning Catalina to sit near him. "Please take a seat in the padded chair. It's the best we have."

Chairs were arranged in a semicircle facing the fireplace. The smell of burning pine needles, bark, and smoke filled the air. A quiet tension settled in the room.

Catalina glanced from face to face, five men and Marie. Everyone leaned into the fire, rubbing hands chilled by the night. No one spoke.

Edouard broke the silence. *"Pardonnez-nous,* Catalina. Few people seek us out. We're always in danger, and you're wanted by the Gestapo. It's risky to bring you here."

"I'm sorry," she said. "Perhaps I shouldn't have come." Shaking, she placed her cup on the floor and cradled her hands in her lap—wringing them. Lorenzo told her to find the *Maquis.* But was this what she wanted? "I might put your mission at risk. I'll leave in the morning."

The men exchanged glances.

"Catalina," Edouard continued, "we didn't intend to frighten you away. Please, let us introduce ourselves. Tomorrow we'll discuss how you might help. You must know, what we do is very dangerous. Perhaps … um … this is not what you really want."

She picked up her cup. Hands still shaking, she studied the men's faces, waiting for them to start.

"You'll call us by our *nom de guerre,*" Edouard began. "It's the only name you need to know. If you remain with us you'll be known by the name on your papers, Charlotte Beaumont."

She nodded. Would they let her stay? Did she want to fight in the Resistance?

"Each *maquisard* has a specialty—talents we like to call them. Marie, you start."

Marie, a petite woman with short brown hair said, "My *nom de guerre* is Marie Leclair. I'm a courier. I share information about the Germans with *Maquis* cells along the Riviera. It's dangerous but the *Boches* are less likely to suspect a woman." Almost without emotion she added, "The Gestapo killed my parents because they wouldn't work as collaborators. They died protecting us. They didn't give in to the Germans. I'm proud of them." As she finished she reached over and took Edouard's hand.

He gives her strength. Are they lovers? Charlotte wondered.

Edouard added, "You know my real name, but call me Rémi Montagne. You remember my parents, I'm sure. They're safe—hidden and confined because of my work. We don't communicate very often. It's too risky. But my father accumulates information and sends it to me every three to four months. He supports our war efforts, too. He always includes money with his letters. Tomorrow we'll show you how notes are passed, so Germans can't intercept."

Charlotte nodded and rubbed her eyes, exhaustion setting in.

"One more introduction. The rest can wait until tomorrow. Théo is our youngest. Only nineteen. He is daring, a risk-taker," Edouard smiled.

Théo laughed as he leaned in to speak. "I'm not that courageous. Rémi exaggerates. Before the war, I studied engineering. Now I am an expert in explosives. I destroy instead of build. So far I've only lost one finger." He held up his hand. "Just a little one. A badge of courage," he said, sitting back down.

Charlotte smiled at him. Tall and thin with icy blue eyes, he was very cute, even without a finger.

***

Charlotte woke to the sound of people talking in the adjoining room. She'd been sleeping on the floor, next to an inside wall. Rolling over onto her knees, she cupped her hands around her ear and leaned against the wall. She could only make out a word or two at a time, but she could tell they were talking about her. Most argued for her to stay. Only one disagreed. He wanted to send her back to Nice.

A rustling sounded at the door. She slumped into the blankets and closed her eyes. Marie slipped into the room, closed the door, and walked quietly toward Charlotte. Shaking her by the shoulder, she whispered, "Get up. Quickly. Defend yourself. The men are deciding your fate."

Charlotte's eyes popped open. Rolling to her side, she propped herself up on one elbow. "What can I say?"

"I know these men," Marie said. "They're good, but must reduce risk. Few women join the *Maquis*, and you are a foreigner. Convince them you can be useful. They need someone to translate correspondence from the *Maquis* in Menton. They speak good Italian, but terrible French. If you translate—then messages will be clearer."

Marie stopped, listened, and continued, "We also need a second woman to sit in the cafés and pick up local news. There are rumors of an Allied invasion in the north of France. We need the truth. Café patrons speak French, Italian, and German. Can you speak German too?"

Catalina nodded. "I'm not fluent in German, but I understand it and speak a little."

Rémi knocked and entered the room. "Ah, you are awake. Freshen up, then come out and join us for breakfast. We're making plans." He winked at Marie, turned, and left the room.

***

In the kitchen, Charlotte cupped water with her hands from a tiny bowl and splashed it on her face. Filling a small glass with fresh water, she rinsed her mouth and spat. She'd slept in her clothes. Later, she would ask where to bathe.

Marie handed her a hard roll and a cup of light brown liquid that smelled faintly of coffee. Charlotte carried her breakfast into the dining room and took a seat at the table.

"Charlotte," Rémi said, "the men want to know what skills you have. And we need to understand why you made the journey from Torino to Nice. It's a very dangerous thing to do. Few people would take the risk."

Make this good or you could be back in Nice by

nightfall, Charlotte cautioned herself. She took a deep breath and began. "My parents despise Mussolini, especially after he joined the Axis powers. My brother Pietro was forced into the army. When the Allies took Sicily and began to move up the Italian peninsula, Pietro deserted and went into hiding."

Charlotte shuddered, remembering Pietro's contorted body and the blood-soaked snow. "When the Germans began moving south to keep the Allies from reaching Rome, my parents feared for my safety. They sent me to Nice to stay with my aunt and uncle. When I arrived, I saw German soldiers milling around their home—like mosquitos buzzing for fresh blood. I suspected something horrible, so I returned to Old Nice, without making contact."

"My name is Patrick," a man said. His eyes were dark brown, and his hair black, like Edouard's. "How can you be certain no one followed you?"

"I spent time in the cafés, hoping to make contact with Edouard, uh, Rémi. No one approached me. I watched carefully."

Rémi nodded.

"I can help you," Charlotte offered. "I am fluent in Italian and French, and I know some German. I have a good memory. When I hear a conversation I remember what was said, word-for-word. I can also ride a bicycle—very fast if I have to. Eighty kilometers a day, even if the terrain is rough or steep. In Torino, I delivered messages to families in hiding. I was often their only means of communication."

She paused to dip a chunk of roll into her coffee. "My brother, Pietro, was slaughtered by the Germans on the trail to Menton. So young....," she swallowed hard. "They didn't have to kill him. They could have taken him prisoner."

"We heard about it," Rémi said. "But I didn't know Pietro was among them. I'm very sorry. I remember him well."

Charlotte nodded, drew a sharp breath, and sat up straight. "A few days after Pietro was killed, my guide was murdered by a Nazi assassin. I killed the *Boche* with my brother's knife. I carry his dagger." She patted her skirt. "It's my talisman, and I'm not afraid to use it."

A tall well-tanned man stood and leaned against the wall. "My name is Robin. Sometimes we kill because there is no choice. It's either you or them. So, I'd like to know—do you think you can kill again, or will you shy away from it? Put yourself at risk, and us too?"

Charlotte glared. "Are you questioning my will? My love for my brother—my country?" She felt her cheeks flush, and her mouth go dry. Avenging her brother was her sole ambition. She had to convice them.

"It's not easy to kill...." Robin said. "That's all I meant."

Rémi glanced around the room. "We need your talents, Charlotte. I think everyone agrees."

Robin nodded.

All of them smiled, except one. Théo beamed.

"Patrick and Jules, introduce yourselves. Then we'll have Charlotte begin training. Théo, you'll help her with throwing knives and shooting a gun."

"I took a pistol from my guide's body. I want to use his gun," Charlotte said.

"*Certainement,*" Rémi replied, a pleased look flashing across his face. He whispered to Marie. "She is full of surprises," Charlotte heard. "Her escape from Italy hardened her. She'll be able to help us."

Chapter 10
A Quarry near Falicon

"We use knives because they don't require ammunition. They're lethal if you hit the right spot, and ... they're quiet," Théo said, smiling. "I'll train you to throw, but it takes a lot of practice, something you'll need to do every day. Your life depends on accuracy."

They stood at the bottom of a quarry, a large log with a bull's-eye painted on it was the enemy. While hiking, Théo explained why they'd chosen such a desolate place to practice.

"We don't want the sounds to carry," he said. "The quarry sends sound up rather than out to any Germans who might prowl the woods. If we have time, we'll practice shooting, too."

Charlotte nodded.

"Now, take off your coat. It's always hot at the bottom of this pit and you'll need the full motion of your arms. First rule: if you think you'll need a knife, make certain it's accessible. You don't want clothes getting in the way."

She draped her coat over a large boulder. Théo threw his on top.

"We all carry two knives, in sheaths at the small of our back."

He handed her two sheaths. "Lace your belt through the loops on the backside of the sheath, just like mine." He turned around. "See how snugly they fit?"

She swallowed hard. "Umm, I don't have a belt. I use the waistband of my skirt to hold Pietro's knife. Will that work for these too?"

"No. You need something more, and keep the sheaths at your back, not your side. You want to look unarmed," Théo said. "I have some rope. You can use that for now, then we'll get you a belt." Théo pulled a length of rope from his rucksack. "Here, I'll lace the sheaths onto the rope, and tie it around you."

"I can do it," Charlotte said, pulling away. "I'm good at tying knots. If I tie them, I can untie them." She worried about the diamonds. He might feel them.

Théo watched her slip the rope through the sheaths, then tie it around her waist. "How's this?" she asked, turning around.

"Uh, it's fine," he said with a questioning glance. "Good enough for today."

Had she made him suspicious? Charlotte wondered. She'd promised her father to protect the necklace. That meant keeping it a secret, from *everyone.*

"You have a good eye," Théo told her, after practicing for an hour. "Good balance too. You throw best when gripping the handle, not the blade. The snap of your wrist is strong and true. Are you sure you've never done this before?"

She smiled. "Maybe a little. Still, it's difficult for me to reach back for the knife. My motions need to be smoother and quicker."

Théo smiled. "You want to be the next White Fox?"

Charlotte grinned. "She's legendary. We heard about her in Italy. She often led men to safety over the Alps. Maybe I should change my *nom de guerre* to *Le Chat Blanc?"*

Théo laughed. "You never can tell what the war will bring."

The day was warming. "Let's get out of the sun. Marie prepared some food. Grab your coat and we'll head up there, under the trees." He pointed just beyond the edge of the quarry.

Charlotte followed him over the boulder field, then suddenly stopped. Memories of Rafael flooded through her. He'd helped move the rock that pinned her leg, and now he was gone. Forever. Her knees shook and she began to sway.

"What is it? Sit down. Here. Now." Théo motioned to a large rock.

"This awful war," she choked. "In a month's time I've lost my brother, my guide, and probably my aunt and uncle. And now, *I* train to kill."

"We can't abandon our nation—our families and friends. We've chosen to fight back," Théo said. "Drive these murderers from our soil. Forever."

She closed her eyes, wishing it all away. But the memories persisted.

Chapter 11
Planning Sabotage
Falicon

Charlotte and Théo entered the farmhouse in the late afternoon. A cast-iron pot teeming with vegetables simmered at the edge of the fireplace. Her stomach growled so loudly everyone looked up as she entered. She clutched her belly and chuckled. "I can't hide it. My stomach tells the truth. I'm so hungry I could eat stale bread!"

Laughter filled the room.

"Marie," Charlotte said, "now that there is another woman in the house you must let me help."

Marie answered with a smile. "The table needs setting, but the men will have to move their planning elsewhere. Our dining room has many uses."

"Shall I shoo them away, or do they take a subtle hint?" Charlotte asked.

"The women have taken over. One was hard enough, but now we have two!" Rémi said, gesturing at the *maquisards* to pick up their papers and move.

Charlotte set the table with their best china—chipped plates, nothing matching. She stood back, frowning, then turned and left the house.

Within minutes, she was back with a bouquet of juniper. "Marie, do you have something we can put these in?"

"But of course. We're civilized," she said with a wink.

Charlotte popped the greenery into a white vase. The porcelain glaze, covered with tiny hairline cracks, was chipped at the base. But Charlotte thought it beautiful. A touch of home.

"Help me serve the soup," Marie requested. "There is bread on the table. We're ready to eat."

Conversation was light and easy during dinner. Charlotte felt herself fitting in. What a gift to have found the *Maquis*.

After dinner, the women cleaned up while the men pulled chairs to the fireplace and began another round of planning. She could see life taking on a certain pattern: eat, sleep, plan attacks, practice. Charlotte wondered about the missions. How do they pull them off without getting caught? The *Maquis* were known for their guerrilla warfare, she reminded herself. They had the answers.

Charlotte and Marie joined the men around the hearth.

Rémi led the discussion. "*Maquis* cells will be coordinating attacks on trains—in particular those moving south from Paris to the Mediterranean coast, and along the Côte d'Azur. They'll be carrying German soldiers, guns, and munitions. For maximum effect, we'll strike at the same time on the same day."

"Why the mass movement?" Marie asked.

"Our friends in the cafés report Hitler fears a coordinated Allied attack. The Führer," Rémi spat on the floor, "knows Churchill wants to invade the 'soft underbelly of Europe'—starting in Italy and moving north. If the Allies succeed, they could be on the Austrian border within a few months. But, the Germans also suspect a second attack—this one in the southern coast of France, or in the north, near Calais.

"Robin is our wireless operator," Rémi said, glancing at Charlotte. "A dangerous job. The Germans find and murder most operators within six months. So far, luck has held. Keep him in your prayers."

"The railway attacks are planned for a week from today," Robin added. "We hope to do enough damage to stop all train movement for several weeks—cutting off German supplies and manpower to the south. Each cell must decide on the best place to attack."

"We're looking for a small village," Rémi told Charlotte, "something west of Cannes."

Charlotte nodded. "But why wouldn't we sabotage a train coming through Nice? Seems easier, it's so close."

"We don't want our cell to be identified with the sabotage," Rémi said. "Nice is highly patrolled. If seen near the rails, we could put the Germans on alert. Then they'd place guards on every mile of track and the mission would fail."

"Patrick and I will pinpoint the location," Robin said. "We want a site where there's a sharp turn in the tracks and a steep cliff on the Mediterranean side."

Théo explained, "There's no need to waste explosives when we can use geography to our advantage. Before the train comes through, we'll unbolt the connection plates on the outside rail. When the engine crosses the plate, it gives way. The entire train should cascade into the sea. Everything is lost—cars, soldiers, and cargo."

"If any Germans survive the wreck," Patrick said, "Jules will be positioned on a cliff overlooking the site, ready to pick them off. The rest of us help, but he is our expert marksman."

Charlotte gulped audibly. The sabotage meant vengeance on a mass scale. She hadn't considered this. Goose bumps rose on her arms and a shiver rippled across her shoulders. She wondered what her parents would say. She hoped they'd be proud.

"We're all tired," Rémi said. "We'll talk more in the morning. Marie, please show Charlotte her new room."

"Not where I was last night?" she asked.

"There are only three bedrooms," Marie said. "We have three men in one, two in another, and Rémi and I in the third. We'll put you in the room with only two men. It's large and we've hung a little curtain for privacy."

"That's very nice," Charlotte said, blushing. "Pietro and I shared a room when we were young. This is not so different. We are all family, *oui*?" She glanced around the room. "So, who are my new brothers?"

Jules's face lit up with a broad grin. Théo bit his lip, and glanced at the floor.

Chapter 12
A Spy in the Making
Riviera

The next morning, Charlotte found Marie alone in the kitchen.

"Help yourself to brioche and a cup of coffee," Marie told her. "Let's sit by the fire. I'd like to talk with you."

The women pulled chairs up to the hearth and sat, cradling breakfast in their laps.

"Today we're fortunate," Marie said. "Our neighbor gave us a dozen brioches. She is a magnificent cook and very generous."

"Umm, this *is* delicious," Charlotte said, biting off a section of the roll.

"Do you know the story of Marie Antoinette and brioche? My mother told it to me a hundred times." Marie laughed.

"But of course. Everyone's heard the English translation of the queen's famous quote, 'Let them eat cake.' The English mistook 'brioche' for 'cake.' The queen really said, 'Let them eat brioche'!"

"It's such a silly story, but I enjoy it every time." Marie sighed. "It reminds me of my mother."

Glancing at Marie, Charlotte placed her cup on the floor. How awful to lose both parents in the war. She hoped her mother and father were safe, back in Torino.

"So, what do you need to tell me? I'm very curious," Charlotte said.

"Since you will join me in Nice, gathering information in the cafés, we must change your appearance. Rémi reminded us of the flyers that are circulating about you. The Gestapo's work."

Charlotte shook her head. "Hard to believe I'm that important."

"They believe you killed one of their top assassins, and they're determined to find you. I've seen the flyers. I wouldn't have guessed their clumsy sketch was you, but we still need to take it seriously." Marie took a deep breath. "This is what I have in mind—trim your hair and dye it. What do you think?"

Charlotte jerked to attention, her eyes wide.

"I'll loan you scarves and berets, a different dress, too, and a coat." Marie nervously tore off a piece of brioche.

"Don't worry," Charlotte said. "I'm not so vain that I'd risk my life and the lives of the Falicon *Maquis* for the color or length of my hair. Let's finish breakfast, then you can turn me into a blonde!"

***

An empty bottle of peroxide rested on the kitchen counter. Long clips of dark tresses cluttered the floor. Marie stood at the sink, shampooing and rinsing Charlotte's hair. Finally, she stepped back and handed Charlotte a towel.

"Back to the fireplace. I'll brush your hair as it dries. It shouldn't take long now that it's trimmed. We are all curious about your new look," Marie said.

"My hair feels wonderful. You could have dyed it green and I wouldn't have cared. It hasn't been *really* clean since I left Italy," Charlotte said.

When Charlotte's hair was dry, Marie inspected the result and smiled. "It's quite nice," she said. "Now stay right there. I'll fetch a mirror."

Charlotte felt her hair. It barely touched her shoulders. Marie must have cut off thirty centimeters. Two or three years' growth. It's only hair, she scolded herself.

Marie approached with a small mirror. "Here, take a look. It's very cute."

Charlotte gasped, pressing her hand to her lips. "I look so different. Even my parents wouldn't recognize me. Marie, you're an artist!"

Distracted from their meeting, Rémi and Théo glanced at the women.

"Ah!" cried Rémi. "You could be the new pin-up girl, or how do they say…bombshell?"

"I think I'm falling in love," mumbled Théo.

Charlotte glanced at Théo and blushed. Had she heard right?

"If it weren't for my Marie, you'd have to fight me for her," Rémi said with a grin. "But I love Marie more than life itself."

***

The two women spent the morning in Nice. They stopped at three different cafés. Each time Marie pointed out both known collaborators and legitimate contacts—those that could be trusted with information.

"*Maquis* cells keep tabs on collaborators," Marie said in a whisper. "We learn to recognize them. They often frequent the cafés, trying to listen in on conversations."

Marie continued, "*Maquisards* share information three different ways. Sometimes one is safer or more direct than another. We use message couriers, wireless, and casual meetings in cafés. Without accurate news, we would never be effective in our attacks—in fact, many more of us would lose our lives."

The women strolled arm-in-arm along the Promenade des Anglais, the sound of gentle waves washing the pebbled beach. The air was cool, the sun bright, and the sky clear. A beautiful fall day.

"Now that you've seen how we work the cafés," Marie said. "I'll explain how we exchange written messages. The notes are very short. We have designated drop-off places."

"Sounds dangerous," Charlotte said. "The sites could be watched."

"Yes. So never write more than is necessary. One sentence at most. We change the sites regularly. One week it might be at the base of a fence post, the next in an orchard near a specific tree, then behind a loose stone in a wall. We can't become predictable. That's when we're caught or the information is compromised, and lives lost."

"How do you know the secret locations?" Charlotte asked.

"New drop-off sites are often communicated by wireless."

Charlotte sighed. "Am I ready for this? It's complicated. I'll need to practice."

"Don't worry. We'll work together, until you are ready to run messages on your own."

"Thank you," said Charlotte, pulling closer to Marie. "I don't want to fail."

"You won't. Now, let's go back to Falicon. We'll have some stale bread and then you can work with your knives."

Charlotte laughed. Teasing her seemed to be a way of life with the *Maquis*.

Chapter 13
Learning to Kill
Falicon

Théo was waiting for Charlotte when she returned. "We have a few more hours of light. There's a clearing in the woods where we can practice."

A brisk wind blew as they reached the clearing. An eerie mist skimmed the ground, threading its fingers through the trees. Charlotte breathed on her hands, warming them.

"Don't you have gloves?" Théo asked.

She shook her head. "I lost them somewhere between Torino and Nice."

"Ah, well, there's no going back for them," Théo said, laughing.

Charlotte shook her head. Théo was funny *and* cute. Maybe he'll be more than a colleague. I've never had a boyfriend.

"Marie has extra gloves. Be sure to ask for a pair," Théo said.

"Now for our lesson. We won't throw knives today. Instead, you'll practice *retrieving* them from your small-of-the-back sheaths. Your technique needs to be quick and sure. Stand next to me and mimic my movements. You'll work without the sheaths and knives at first. Do you see that tree across the way? The one with the yellowing leaves?"

Charlotte nodded.

"Sight on the oak. I'll demonstrate in slow motion."

Théo stood facing the tree. His sheaths were positioned in a "V" against his back. He reached around his waist with his right hand and grabbed the handle of a knife, then took a stance and prepared to throw.

"Now, once more, but rapidly," he said, executing the action.

"So fast!" Charlotte gasped.

"You'll learn. Remember how I instructed?"

"Of course," Charlotte said. "Face forward, retrieve the knife, grip it like a hammer."

"*Oui*. Now do that."

Charlotte followed his instructions.

"Good. What comes next?" Théo prodded.

"I hold my arm straight out and prepare to throw. Like this," she said, "then angle my hand skyward, keeping my eye on the target, and throw the blade hard and fast."

He smiled. "Good. Now watch me again. You must be very quick. Your opponent may have a gun."

All she saw was a blur.

"Any questions?" Théo asked.

"Uh, no. I'll need a lot of practice, though." She blew on her hands and rubbed her palms together.

Théo smiled. "It may be cold, but it's better to throw without gloves."

"I'll remember that in the dead of winter," she said, with a smile.

Théo pulled her sheaths from his rucksack. They were strung on a belt.

"Today you graduate to a belt—no more rope. Stand still and I'll buckle it around you."

Charlotte stiffened. He was sure to feel the necklace, wrapped around her waist.

"I can do it," she insisted.

Ignoring her, he pulled Pietro's knife from her waistband and tucked it into his belt.

"Stop squirming," he said, struggling to thread the belt around her. Finally, he had it laced through the buckle and pulled it tight.

"Ouch!" Charlotte complained when the belt pushed the diamonds into her back.

"What's the matter?" he asked.

"Nothing. Please, show me what to do next," she said, adjusting the belt.

He stood back—brows furrowed. "I don't like secrets. Do you carry something that will put us at risk?"

"No. You pulled it too tight. Let's practice," she insisted.

Théo scowled and took a deep breath but didn't persist. "Follow my movements. First slow motion, then a little faster each time."

They worked for about an hour—pulling the knives from one side and then the other.

"Your motions are smooth. Good work. Tomorrow we'll go to the quarry and practice throwing at a target."

Charlotte nodded, wondering if his suspicions had faded.

"Now, I'll show you how to use your dagger. You killed the German who took your guide's life—but you did it out of fear and vengeance. You need training to kill quickly and silently—every time. Watch me," he said.

"One way to kill is a technique taught by the British. Approach from behind. Wrap your left arm around his neck, pull him backwards into you, and drive your knife into his chest. This is difficult for a woman. You need strength to press your knife through his clothing and deep into his chest.

"There is a second way to kill...."

Théo glanced at Charlotte. She stared back at him, eyes wide—skin white and waxen. She felt her head buzz and her vision dim. The last thing she remembered before the world turned black was Théo catching her.

"Charlotte, Charlotte!" She'd collapsed on the ground. Théo patted her cheeks lightly. "Wake up."

Who is Charlotte? She wondered, then remembered. Taking a shallow breath, she opened her eyes. "Oh, Théo. What happened? Did I faint? That's never happened before."

He pulled her to a sitting position. "I'll get water."

He retrieved his canteen. Holding it to her lips, he encouraged her to drink.

Feeling queasy, she waved him off.

Théo pulled her to his chest, holding her tightly.

"I killed the Nazi," she gasped. "Slashed his throat with Pietro's knife. I never cried. I was glad. Please don't think me weak."

"I don't think you're weak at all. But it's getting dark. The others will worry. Let's go back. We'll talk later."

He touched her gently on the face. "Come," he said, pulling her up.

They walked together, holding hands. The smell of soup again filled the house, reviving Charlotte's spirits. She hung her coat near the door and walked into the kitchen, ready to help.

"You look pale. Your cheeks should be rosy. It's cold outside," Marie said. "Is something wrong?"

Charlotte shivered.

"Sit near the window," Marie said. "Let's talk."

"I killed a man. You know that. Practicing with knives brought it back." Charlotte drew in a deep breath. "I want to be brave, but the memory haunts me."

Rémi walked into the room. "Dinner almost ready?"

Marie glanced at him and shook her head.

His brow furrowed when she waved him back.

"I know the men are hungry," Charlotte said. "I'll be okay in a few minutes."

"Take your time. Let them eat bread," Marie said,

with a smile.

Patting her cheeks to give them some color, Charlotte stood and gathered up the dinner plates. "I'll set the table," she said. "I'm okay."

***

Charlotte slipped away soon after dinner. She was tired and wanted to be alone. Entering the bedroom she shared with Jules and Théo, Charlotte pulled on her nightgown, climbed into bed, and was soon asleep.

Hours later she woke. Lying quietly, Charlotte listened for the village clock to chime. Within a few moments it rang twice. The bell was comforting.

She got out of bed, opened the door, and walked to the living room. Dying embers warmed the hearth. Snuggling into the big chair in front of the fireplace, she let her mind drift to her parents and home. Crossing herself, she whispered a little prayer. Surely they'll survive this horrible war.

The bedroom door opened and closed. Théo pulled up a chair next to hers.

"How do you feel?" he asked.

"Fine. Please don't worry about me."

He drew his chair closer, reached over, and took her hand. Théo's palm was calloused and rough, but warm.

"You're kind," Charlotte said, turning to him.

"*Maquisards* help each other. We're family. For some—like Marie—we are the *only* family. She cares for you like a sister."

Sighing, Charlotte tried to move closer to Théo.

"Let me squeeze into the big chair. I want to hold you," Théo said.

She rested her head on his shoulder. His breathing grew short. Then his lips were on hers and a warmth flooded through her, filling her with emotions she'd never felt before.

Hesitantly, she pulled away, whispering, "My first kiss."

The fire illuminated his face. He looked surprised.

"Really? The first? But you're so beautiful, and certainly old enough to, uh—kiss."

"My parents were extremely protective. They would not want me here with the *Maquis*, in a bedroom with two men."

Théo cleared his throat. "Err, yes, I understand."

Charlotte giggled. "No, I don't think you do. But I have a favor to ask."

"*Oui?*"

"Kiss me again."

Chapter 14
A Messenger
Riviera

Charlotte gulped hard as she listened to Marie. Was she ready for this?

"Today's assignment is more dangerous and a lot more strenuous than yesterday's," Marie said. "You'll deliver and pick up written messages. I'll go with you, in case you run into trouble, but this is *your* mission."

Marie placed a small hand-drawn map on the dining table. "The circles mark the latest *Maquis* message centers, along the Riviera. These little notes," Marie held one up, "supply information to all cells in southern France."

Charlotte drew closer as Marie pointed at the map. "Here we are, and this is where you need to go." She ran her finger from Falicon to Nice, then along the coast to St-Laurent-du-Var. "We'll travel by bicycle. It's only twenty kilometers. The difficult part is returning from Nice to Falicon—seven kilometers, straight uphill.

"Be careful that no one follows you. Sometimes I slip into the trees and wait to see if anyone is coming. We can't risk exposing our cell. Also, remember the Nazi curfew is sunset."

"I'll be cautious. Biking won't be a problem. In Italy, I delivered milk and eggs from our farm to the markets."

"Good. We'll leave in a few hours. We want to blend in with others who are headed for the market in Old Nice. I'll be about fifty meters behind you," Marie said. "You'll deliver and retrieve messages. The folding of the note is important. It's one way to tell if it's authentic. The message you retrieve must be folded exactly like the one you deliver. I'll demonstrate in a minute. If you arrive in St-Laurent and don't find a message, the site may have been compromised. Leave immediately."

Charlotte swallowed hard and took in a deep breath. "Where will I find the message?"

"The pick-up site is a small courtyard on the grounds of L'Eglise Saint-Laurent. Leave your bike at the entrance to the church. Take the side door on your left, and go to the inner courtyard. Look for the smallest palm tree. Tucked in a loose section of bark, on the north side of the tree, you'll find a note. Remove it and leave the one I've given you. I'll be across the street. Do *not* look for me. Just know that I'm there."

"Won't it look strange if I ride into St-Laurent, and immediately turn around and go back to Nice?" Charlotte asked.

"Now you're thinking like a *maquisard*," Marie said, smiling. "I'll give you some francs. There's a small market near the center of the village. See, here on the map," she pointed. "Buy some vegetables and meat, if they have any. Place the packages in your bicycle basket and return to Falicon. Remember, you must be home before curfew."

***

The women left Falicon at 10h00 in the morning. Their old battered bikes sped down the hill to Nice. The November wind left Charlotte's cheeks red and hands stinging. The sun hung low in the sky—rays skimming the dark waters of the Mediterranean. The *mistrals* would soon arrive, bringing relentless winds and bitter cold rains.

Charlotte and Marie entered Nice at Place de Garibaldi. Stopping to catch her breath, Marie said, "When you're ready, go ahead. I'll follow behind."

The Promenade des Anglais was easy riding, but at the western end where Charlotte left the concrete walkway, the path became a patchwork of disrepair—pockmarked and crumbling.

Shortly after noon, Charlotte entered the city limits of St-Laurent. A web of narrow disconnected streets made finding the church difficult. The city, designed according to the old medieval "cow paths," had no grid plan. Many roads ended in cul-de-sacs.

Charlotte finally saw the bell tower, high above the sanctuary. Propping her bike against the exterior wall, she slipped through the door into the courtyard. She found the smallest palm tree and looked for misaligned bark. "There it is," she mumbled, pulling back the husk. The paper folds were identical. She exchanged messages just as the church bells sounded, 13h00.

Charlotte exited the church and picked up her bike. Marie wasn't visible, but she said she'd be close by. Charlotte arrived at the market as sellers were packing up. Little food remained. One stand had a few carrots, small potatoes, and apples. The owner chatted and sipped coffee with another woman.

Purchases made, Charlotte dropped the bag into the bike basket, patted her coat pocket where she'd slipped the new message, and set out for Nice.

A gray haze masked the sun, reminding Charlotte that only three hours of sunlight remained. She watched for the road back to the Promenade but the winding, unmarked streets confused her. Charlotte took the first major road left, an unmarked route east.

She soon realized it was the wrong road. The sea should be on her right. At the next intersection, Charlotte turned south, hoping to connect with the Promenade. Cars honked and tires screeched. She jumped the curb, trying to avoid a car. The bike's rear wheel caught on a newspaper stand. The bicycle twisted awkwardly, and Charlotte tumbled onto the sidewalk.

An elderly man reached down to help her. A teenage girl gathered the spilled produce. Knees bloodied and her coat torn, Charlotte's only concern was for the message. She slipped her hand into her pocket, touching the note with her fingertips. Safe.

"Your handlebars are twisted," said a voice from behind. "I can fix them." A young man took the front wheel between his knees and pressed the bars into alignment. "There, that should do it. Be careful on these one-way streets. You could be lost for weeks if you take a wrong turn," he said, laughing.

"*Merci*. You're very kind," Charlotte said.

"Where are you headed?" asked the young man.

"Not far. I know my way now. *Merci beaucoup,*" she said, trying not to sound anxious. Too many questions.

Her hands shook as she walked the bike down the sidewalk. The young man caught up. "If you'd like a ride, I have a car. We can tie the bike on the back."

"No, no. I'm fine." She turned down a side street, hoping he wouldn't follow, but he did.

"You forgot your vegetables," he said, placing them in her basket.

"Oh, thank you," Charlotte said.

"Your bike appears to have seen better days. I am happy to drive you wherever you like."

"Please, I must be going. My parents are waiting for me. *Au revoir*." She turned away and mounted the bike. The clouds had moved off and the sun was beginning to set. She headed south, back to the Promenade.

Marie slipped in beside Charlotte. "What happened? Once you reached the market I headed back to the Promenade. I thought you were safe. Where have you been?" She looked Charlotte up and down. "Oh, your knees...."

"I'll be okay. It's late—we need to hurry. I got lost. Can we travel together now?" Charlotte asked.

"Of course. Follow me," Marie said.

***

Charlotte limped along, as Marie tried to guide both bikes up the hill. The going was slow. "It's beyond curfew," Charlotte said. "What if we're stopped?"

"Don't worry. We're almost to the farmhouse. And look ahead!" Marie said. "Théo and Rémi are coming down the hill. They'll help us."

"What happened?" Rémi asked, taking Marie's bike. Théo took Charlotte's.

"I hit a curb and fell off my bike," Charlotte said. "I feel so silly. My first mission," she shook her head. "But I did get the message," she said proudly.

"We can talk later," Rémi cautioned. "Our voices carry."

Charlotte wondered if she was smart enough to be a spy. She sighed loudly. Théo reached over and took her hand. "Don't worry," he said. "You won't make the same mistake again."

Chapter 15
Planning Sabotage
Falicon

After dinner Rémi gathered the *maquisards* around the dining table. Charlotte was still embarrassed about crashing her bike on the way home. She didn't feel part of the group. She'd have to prove herself.

"We have three days to prepare the derailment of the German train," Rémi said. "Patrick, where is the best place to unbolt the tracks?"

"Robin, Jules, and I have settled on a good site. One kilometer east of St-Rafael, the most vulnerable point. The train has the steepest fall and the tracks run very close to the sea. There'll be few survivors," Patrick said, "if any."

Charlotte hoped her earlier fiasco wouldn't keep her from participating in the new mission.

"I remember San Rafaël," Charlotte said. "Our parents used to take us there. It's right on the sea—beautiful."

"*Oui*. That was then. Now, we are at war, with sabotage on our minds," Rémi said.

Charlotte glanced at Marie. Was Rémi trying to make her sound silly? Was he dismissive?

Marie shook her head, ever so slightly. Perhaps he is just under pressure, Charlotte thought. Don't take it personally.

Rémi turned to Jules. "Where should we position ourselves?"

"I've picked a place for each of us on the hill overlooking the tracks. We have enough rifles for everyone, and plenty of bullets," Jules said.

Robin added, "I'll check the wireless every day before the attack, to make certain it is a 'go' for the *Maquis*. Last minute coordination."

"Charlotte and Marie, I want you to visit the cafés in Nice. There is sure to be talk. An hour each day should do," Rémi said.

"In advance of the attack I want everyone to practice shooting," Rémi added. "Our goal is to kill all survivors. No prisoners. Also, sharpen your knives and practice throwing. That means everyone," he said, glancing around the room.

"Marie and Théo, work with Charlotte."

In other words, thought Charlotte, he thinks I need extra help. I'd better not disappoint. He's got me on a short leash.

***

"Marie, here's your rifle. And yours, Charlotte." Théo handed each of the women a gun. "British Lee-

Enfields. Thank God the Brits have been able to make their air-drops. No fancy ammo belts, but we have cross-chest *musettes*. You can easily reach into the bag, grab a clip, and reload. Each clip holds five rounds. You can load two clips at a time—one after the other. Ten shots. Then reload. Let's head up to the quarry for practice."

Théo demonstrated how to hold, load, and fire the guns. The *maquisards* stood about thirty meters from the target.

"Okay, Marie, you go first." He watched her lift the gun, hold the butt against her shoulder, take aim, and fire. She hit the outer ring.

"Bravo!" said Charlotte.

On her fifth shot, Marie hit the center.

"Oh my," Charlotte said. "You're good."

Marie stepped a few feet away and motioned Charlotte to take her turn.

Théo stood by Charlotte, positioning her arms. Left hand holding the rifle and the right on the trigger. "Good form. Now shoot."

She braced the gun against her right shoulder, closed her left eye, aimed, and pulled the trigger.

Théo's jaw dropped, and Marie cheered. She'd hit a perfect bull's-eye.

"Beginner's luck," Charlotte said, with a grin.

A second firing put a bullet in the second ring.

"Shoot the next three in succession, Théo said. "Don't pause to position, just bang them out."

"Okay," Charlotte said.

Bam, bam, bam. One in the outer ring, and two in the smallest. Charlotte relaxed her stance and raised an eyebrow at Théo.

"Okay, 'fess up. You've fired a rifle before, haven't you?" Marie said.

Charlotte smiled at the opportunity to prove herself. "Papa and I used to hunt deer before the war. He taught me to shoot. There are a few antlers mounted on our barn, and a couple of odd-looking lamps inside the farmhouse."

"You ladies don't need any more gun practice. Let's work on knife throwing. First, retrieve your knife and position to throw. Then release the knife. *Voilà!* Bull's-eye." Théo smiled. "Remember, practice with both right and left hands."

Marie took position, held her breath, and with a blur of motion pulled the blade from its sheath and threw—landing right in the middle ring of the target. Charlotte smiled and nodded. "Nice work."

Marie threw a few more, hitting the inner rings and a bull's-eye.

Charlotte was nearly giddy. The smell of success buoyed her spirits. Throwing knives at a target was more like a game. Memories of Pietro and Rafael didn't torment her as they had previously.

"All right, let's see what Charlotte can do," Théo said.

Charlotte threw, but missed the target, hitting a nearby tree. "Awful!" She tried again, this time hitting the outer ring. "Better," she mumbled, "but not good."

"Both of you, fetch your knives and try again. We don't leave until you both hit the bull's-eye."

Marie was just as talented with right and left hands. Both knives hit the center. She retrieved her knives, resheathed them, and waited for Charlotte to take her turn.

"Keep your eye on the center of the target, even as you reach for your knife," Théo told Charlotte.

She heard a thud. Hit—second ring.

One more try for the center. Make it good, Charlotte cautioned herself. She'd been practicing on her own, and her father had shown her some knife-throwing skills. He used to say, "Imagine the knife in the bull's-eye, and that's where it will go." Yesterday she appeared inept. Today she needed to excel.

In rapid motion, she retrieved the knife, took aim, and threw.

"Bull's-eye!" yelled Marie. "You did it!"

But Charlotte wasn't done yet. She had one more knife—Pietro's. She pulled it from her waistband, held her arm out, and took aim. Then stopped, frozen in place.

"This knife isn't designed to throw, but to stab and slice," she said. "I need practice. Turn around, Théo, so your back is to me." She saw his neck muscles tighten.

"Be careful!" he said.

She nodded. Walking quickly toward him, Charlotte grasped his hair and pulled Théo's head back—her blade poised at his throat. She couldn't show weakness. Swallowing hard, she carefully pulled the blade away, took a deep breath, and stood absolutely still.

Théo turned around. Eyes wide, mouth a thin line. "Let's head back to the farmhouse. You two scare me."

Chapter 16
Train Sabotage
Near Cannes

The burning logs flickered, warming the farmhouse. Rémi spread a large map of the Riviera on the table. Charlotte watched as he traced the course they would travel.

"Memorize the route in case we're separated. We'll drive the back roads to avoid German checkpoints. Should arrive mid-afternoon, then wait for the train. Robin, what have you heard from *Résistance-Fer?*"

"They've organized us well. The *Maquis* are ready. We strike simultaneously at 16h00—throughout southern France."

Rémi nodded. "That's what Charlotte's message said, too. Good confirmation."

"What's *Résistance-Fer?*" she asked.

"The *Fer* specializes in stopping German troop movement and sabotaging trains. They're helping the *Maquis* coordinate attacks," Robin said.

"Will all of us participate?" Charlotte asked, still worried she wouldn't be included.

"Yes, of course. All seven of us. We need everyone," Rémi said.

Charlotte nodded. "Will we take the old truck?"

"Yes. I'll drive," Rémi said. "Patrick in the passenger seat. The rest of you ride in the back section. There is a small curtained window between cab and truck. If it's not too risky, you can look through it—see where we are and what's going on."

"What if we're stopped?" Théo asked.

"I'll play along with their requests," Rémi said. "But I want everyone armed and ready, just in case." He pointed to the map. "When we drop down to the coastal village of Madelieu-La Napule, we're most vulnerable. The Germans patrol frequently. The train tracks and highway run parallel and very close to each other. Ideal for sabotage."

Heads nodded.

Patrick gestured toward the map. "Here, on the coast, when we see the sign that says Calanque de St-Barthélemy, we'll be within one kilometer of the sabotage site."

"Sorry to have so many questions, but what's a '*calanque*'?" Charlotte asked.

"Millions of years ago," Patrick said, "*calanques* were small river valleys that fed into the Mediterranean. The sea was much lower than it is now, with no opening to the Atlantic. The Mediterranean was landlocked."

"I didn't know that," Charlotte said.

Patrick nodded. "When the continents separated, the Atlantic waters moved in, raising the level of the Mediterranean. The *calanques* are what is left of the valleys that once fed into the sea. They filled up. Something like a fjord."

Rémi smiled. "Okay, professor, enough with the geology lesson. Tell us more about the attack."

"I chose our site," Patrick said, "because there's a steep dip in the tracks as the train rounds the corner—traveling east along the sea. The engine will pick up speed just before it hits the connecting plates. Théo and I will unbolt them in advance. When the train hits the plates, the rails separate and the engine careens off the tracks. It'll plunge over the cliff into the sea. No one should survive, but if they do you'll be positioned on the knoll above the cliff—ready to kill anyone who escapes."

"Excellent," Théo agreed.

"Gather your weapons and ammunition," Rémi ordered. "We'll load the truck tonight. In the morning, the local baker delivers boxes of bread and pastries. He'll give us empty boxes too. We'll fill them with straw and rags and stack them in the back of the truck. You can hide behind them, if needed. Any questions?"

The room was silent.

"Be ready at dawn."

Charlotte took a deep breath and exhaled slowly. Nervous energy filled the room.

***

They left at sunrise. The *maquisards* were finally

on a mission, together with all *Maquis* cells in southern France. Charlotte felt the excitement. Hands trembling, she gripped Pietro's knife. He was with her.

They reached Le Cannet, just above Cannes, by 13h00. "The highway exit is just ahead," Rémi said. Charlotte watched through the window.

As they passed through Madelieu-La Napoule, they spotted soldiers posted at a roadblock. German trucks end-to-end.

"We have to stop," Patrick said, alerting everyone in the truck.

Charlotte turned back to the *maquisards*, "The blockade stretches across the avenue. Three German soldiers are waiting."

"Everyone quiet," hissed Rémi.

Charlotte retrieved Pietro's knife.

"Don't you want your rifle?" Théo whispered.

"*Non*. Pietro's knife is enough." She flashed him a determined look.

As the truck slowed to a stop, Charlotte crouched among her companions.

"Two soldiers approaching," Rémi said. "One on each side of the truck. The third is at the roadblock."

Rémi rolled down his window. "*Bonjour, messieurs*."

"*Papiers, bitte. Schnell!*" a soldier ordered.

"Always the '*schnell*'," Patrick mumbled, reaching into his pocket.

"*Papiers!*" the second guard commanded.

Charlotte peeked through a tiny sliver in the

curtained window.

The men handed over their identification. Reading them carefully, the Germans compared pictures and searched for irregularities.

A guard slapped Rémi's papers against the truck, commanding his attention. "What's in the truck?" he demanded, leaning back to read the logo. "Ah, a *boulangerie* on wheels? Ha! The bread must be stale by now," he said, smirking.

Rémi tipped his hand from side to side. "*Non.* Fresh this morning. Want some? I have a box here," he said, reaching behind the seat.

"*Nein!* Don't move! Get out. *I'll* check."

"Both of you, out! *Jetzt!*" commanded the second soldier. "Over here." He held a gun on the two *maquisards.*

Charlotte slipped down to the floor, holding her finger to her lips.

She heard rustling behind Rémi's seat. A box was removed.

Would the soldiers look inside the truck?

Charlotte moved back to the window, watching through a slit in the curtains as the soldier opened the box—freshly baked croissants glistened in the sun.

"The French can go to hell," the German said, biting into a croissant. "But they'll have to leave one baker behind." He laughed.

"Your destination, *bitte*," asked the other soldier.

"We have a delivery in Agay. Finish up in St-Raphaël," Rémi said.

"You won't go anywhere until I've checked inside the truck."

"Oh, God," Charlotte whispered, rubbing her damp palms on her pants.

"Over here," Robin murmured, "behind the boxes." She shifted her weight, sliding over next to the *maquisards*.

The soldiers threw the doors open. A wall of white pastry boxes greeted them. "Pull one out," the *Boche* said.

Some are filled with rags, thought Charlotte. Pray they don't pick one of those.

"Look inside," the soldier ordered.

"Just brioche and small baguettes. Can we keep them?" the young soldier asked.

"Yes, keep them and close the doors. Cars are stacking up."

"Go!" the older German ordered. "Remember, you need to be off the coast road by 15h00. Understand— stupid frog?"

"Uh, yes, we'll hurry. *Merci beaucoup*." Rémi nodded, tapping the brim of his cap.

The soldier at the roadblock waved them around the trucks. A collective sigh of relief rippled through the truck.

"*Mon Dieu*," whispered Charlotte, crossing herself. "Too close...."

When they were well past the roadblock, Rémi began singing the last lines of *La Marseillaise*. "*Aux armes, citoyens, Formez vos bataillons, Marchons,*

marchons!"

***

Charlotte felt the truck slow. "Is this it?" Charlotte asked through the small window.

Patrick nodded. Leaning closer to Rémi, he said, "Drive up the path to your right. Park among the cypress. We'll unload there."

Rémi drove in, cut the motor, and ordered everyone out. "The next train comes through at 15h00. Let it pass. We attack the one that follows, at 16h00. Stuff a few croissants in your pockets. You can eat while you wait. We have more than an hour."

Charlotte shook her head at Marie. "Seems odd. Munching pastries before killing."

"Let's review signals," Rémi said. "When there is imminent danger, the eagle owl makes a shrill call. It sounds like this: *cah, cah, cah.* Quick staccato screeches. The same bird makes a contented cooing—more like an owl in the middle of the night: *who, who, who.* That's the all-clear signal. When you hear it, go back to the truck.

"Marie, get busy painting our new logo, *Casino Supermarchés.*"

"*Oui, monsieur!*" she said, blowing him a kiss. "*Bonne chance, mon amour.*"

"Théo and Patrick, do you have everything you need to unbolt the plates?"

"We're ready," Patrick said, holding up his tools.

Chapter 17
The Eagle Owl Sings
West of Cannes

Charlotte strapped a rifle and *musette* over her shoulder and followed Rémi and Robin. They crouched low as they topped the hill, about thirty meters from the tracks. The steep sides of the *calanque* just beyond—a precipitous drop.

She stretched out on her stomach in the grass, and waited. The 15h00 train came and went. Théo and Patrick unbolted the ties from the plates. It took thirty minutes of cursing and banging to loosen the rusted bolts.

By 16h00 Charlotte had grown tense and stiff. She had no appetite for the bread in her pocket. She just wanted the mission to end ... successfully.

Arrival time came and went. Queasiness roiled in her stomach. Had the Germans gotten wind of the *Maquis* sabotage and delayed the trains?

Then the familiar sound of a locomotive. Rémi and Robin crouched on either side of her, not far away. Muscles on their necks bulged. Charlotte shivered as she readied her rifle. Pietro's knife—tucked in her belt.

The train thundered into sight, accelerating when it hit the downward slope of the tracks, just as Patrick predicted. Then, a terrible screeching. The engine hit the unbolted plates and launched over the cliff. One coach after another vaulted into the *calanque,* leaving two cars perched on the edge of the cliff, the coupler broken. Frothing waters swallowed the engine and forward cars. No one swam ashore.

Charlotte gasped as the doors of the two remaining coaches opened. Dozens of Germans stumbled out. Bloodied and pale with shock, they staggered from the cars. Many stared down into the *calanque.* Like birds atop a fence, they lined up along the railway tracks— some remembered their guns, others not.

The Germans paused a moment. Suddenly, realizing danger, they crouched and ran toward the knoll.

Charlotte heard the eagle owl. Rémi shot twice. Two men fell. He fired again. Charlotte and Robin followed. A young German screamed, clutched his leg, and fell to the ground. A second man was hit in the head. His helmet popped off, toppling into the sea, gray hair soaked with blood.

From Charlotte's left came more shots—Théo and Patrick fired on the soldiers from a different angle. They had little cover—only the *maquis* brush. If anyone fired back, they'd be in trouble.

Again, the cry of an eagle owl. Charlotte glanced around. Germans rushed them from both sides. She took aim but the bolt-action jammed. She worked it again—freeing it up. Rémi fired. A German grabbed his chest and fell. Robin hit another in the thigh. As two more rushed in, Charlotte shouldered her rifle and shot one in the chest and the other in the head. They collapsed within three meters of her, gasping for air—then silent.

She loaded a second clip—her hands shook—her breathing ... ragged.

Seconds later, no Germans were left standing. Cries of wounded filled the air.

One young soldier called for his mother. Did I shoot him? Charlotte wondered. Did Pietro cry for Mama when the Germans killed him? Did he call for me? She swallowed hard, forcing nausea back.

Théo and Robin rose from behind the *maquis*. They fired a few more rounds into the wounded. The crying ceased. Charlotte watched as the two *maquisards* slipped down to the railroad cars and stepped inside.

"Oh, please God, spare our men," she whispered.

Gunshots from inside the train. Then the "all clear" sound of a soft, *who, who who*.

The battle was over.

The *maquisards* gathered on the side of the knoll. Charlotte's legs shook as they jogged back to the truck. She tripped. Théo caught her. "All of them, dead," he said, breathing a sigh of relief. Charlotte took Théo's hand, seeking his strength.

"*Vite*," Patrick motioned. "The train crash and gunshots will bring the *Boches*."

Marie ran to Rémi as he approached the truck. "I was worried," she said. "So much gunfire. Is everyone okay?"

"We're fine, but we've stirred a hornet's nest." Rémi gave her a quick kiss. "Everyone inside!"

Jumping in the driver's seat, Rémi pulled onto the road, first turning north, then west.

The *maquisards* settled in the back. Charlotte glanced at the men. Adrenaline still pumped. She could feel their heat. They celebrated quietly, sharing a bottle of wine.

Charlotte leaned against Théo. "I feel dizzy and sick," she whispered. "I can't stop shaking."

"They were Germans. The enemy," Théo said. "Eat something. It'll help your stomach. There's plenty of bread and wine. Like communion," he said quietly. "Give thanks we're alive and safe."

Breaking the end of a baguette, she took a bite and washed it down with a mouthful of wine.

"I killed a lot of Germans," she whispered, wiping her mouth with the back of her hand. "But I'm not done yet."

***

"There are sure to be roadblocks ahead," Rémi said through the window. "Germans will search every vehicle once word of the sabotage spreads. I'm turning here. We need to stay on side streets."

As they advanced down the dark and meandering

road, Rémi turned the truck's lights off. Their progress slowed to fifteen kilometers an hour. No one spoke.

"A friend of mine lives in Les Adrets-de-l'Estérel," Rémi announced. "Charles supports the *Maquis*, but can't leave his wife and baby to join the *maquisards*. He'll help us find a place for the night, and he might have information on the sabotage."

Rémi pulled between two small cottages and cut the motor. "Stay here."

A knock at the door produced a flutter of curtains. The door opened. "Come in, my friend. Quickly," Charles said, pulling Rémi into the house. The two men embraced. His young wife rocked a baby in the corner. The French Resistance flag hung on the far wall—the tri-colors and Cross of Lorraine.

"I'll brew some tea," Charles said.

"You've heard about the attacks?" Rémi asked.

Charles nodded. "I heard on the wireless. Were you part of that? Bravo. A huge success. But what brings you here?"

"My *maquisards* destroyed a train, killing all the soldiers, near St-Barthélemy. We've been traveling back roads, between villages—working our way home. The coastal roads must be teeming with Germans."

"*Oui*," Charles said. "The *Boches* blocked all highways. You'll need to hide tonight," Charles said. "You can't stay here, but there is an abandoned barn close by. Drive south about two kilometers. When you see a dirt road heading east, take it. You'll see a small barn near a cluster of tall cypress. Pull into the barn and close the doors behind you."

"Do people live there?" Rémi asked.

"No. You'll be safe. How many men do you have?" Charles asked.

"Six others."

"I'll give you bread and a few apples. It's all we have."

"Please keep your food. Let me bring you some baguettes. Our cover was a delivery truck for local cafés," Rémi said.

"Food is hard to come by. My family thanks you."

"*Merci, mon ami*," Rémi said clasping Charles by the shoulders.

"Be careful, my friend."

Chapter 18
Evening: A Day Later
The Falicon Farmhouse

"Falicon is quiet," Charlotte whispered, peeking through the tiny window in the truck.

"That's normal for dusk. Remember the curfew," Patrick said.

"The Nazis will be searching for us," Rémi added, pulling up to the farmhouse. "They could be here ... already."

Patrick leapt out and opened the back doors of the truck.

"Charlotte and Théo, secure the house," Rémi said. "The rest—search the grounds. If anyone sees *anything* suspicious—call out."

"Nothing disturbed here," Charlotte said, moving through the living room.

Théo searched the bedrooms. "No one."

Within an hour the *maquisards* were inside, a fire burning, and biscuits in the oven.

"A toast to Patrick for choosing the perfect sabotage site, *and* a toast to the Falicon *Maquis!*" Charlotte cheered.

Théo lifted his glass. "To more of the same!" Pulling Charlotte close, he kissed her on her cheek.

"She deserves more than a peck. Kiss her like a Frenchman, Théo, or I will!" Jules said, grinning.

"Let's go to the kitchen," Charlotte said, "where we can kiss in private!"

A chorus of laughter followed them—then the clink of glasses and more toasts.

As Charlotte entered the kitchen, Marie handed her a platter of biscuits. "There will be time enough for kissing," she said. "Théo, take the quarter-round of cheese. I'll bring the jam and another bottle of wine."

"Smells wonderful!" Rémi said as the men settled around the table.

"Tomorrow we'll hunt for rabbits," Charlotte said, smiling. "Then we'll have stew."

"There is another reason to celebrate!" Robin said, rushing into the room. "I just checked the wireless. Over two thousand Germans—dead. Ten trains destroyed, and the rails will take weeks to repair."

The *Maquis* cheered—the last of the wine topping off their glasses.

Taking a drink, Charlotte peered over her glass. She was a true *maquisard*—at last. Pietro would be proud, and her parents, too.

After dinner they sat around the fireplace telling jokes and embellishing the mission. She could hear stories taking shape—inflating the truth. Something to confuse historians and delight grandchildren.

Charlotte smiled as Théo took her hand.

The fire burned low. The men excused themselves, one by one. Charlotte and Théo remained—speaking in quiet whispers.

"Earlier, when we were on our way to Falicon, Rémi was very complimentary, but I don't think I deserved it," Charlotte said.

"Of course, you did," Théo said. "I felt safer because you were there—armed and trained. You took out your share of Germans."

"I feel silly asking so many questions, but I'll be a better *maquisard*. So...." She shrugged.

"Whenever you do that shoulder thing, you look so French," Théo smiled.

"I *am* French! Well, half French. Not French enough for you?" she teased.

Théo moved closer. He took her hands in his and said quietly, "You're beautiful, Charlotte. Like no woman I've ever known." He kissed her gently.

Charlotte moaned, shifted her weight, and edged closer. Théo wrapped his arms around her and deepened his kiss.

She pulled away slowly, sighed, and laid her head on his shoulder. When it came to men, Charlotte's parents had been very strict. Holding hands was prohibited, and kissing—well....

"I could sleep in your arms forever," she said, closing her eyes.

"*Mon amour*, a time will come when we can hold each other through the night, but not yet," Théo whispered.

He took Charlotte's hand and led her to the bedroom. She slipped off her shoes, and slid under the blankets. Leaning down, he kissed her once again and whispered, "Tomorrow, we hunt rabbit."

***

The morning sun reflected off the newly fallen snow. Charlotte and Théo stood on the edge of the forest—an expansive meadow to their right.

"Sprinkle the breadcrumbs over here, near the trees," Théo said.

"This is how you hunt rabbits?" She laughed. "You're studying engineering, and this is all you can do? I'd expect a complicated trap. Something mechanical."

"Be careful," he smiled. "I make a big, mean snowball, and *you* make a good target."

She giggled.

"Let's move over there, behind the bushes," he pointed. "Use your knives. A gun is too loud."

Moments passed. "There," Charlotte whispered, pointing. "Let me try...." Slowly, she drew a knife. Her motions were fluid and calculated. Then, a flip of the wrist. The rabbit went down, struggled momentarily, and lay still.

"Good throw!"

"Dinner for one," she smiled.

"A challenge?" Théo asked.

"*Certainement!*"

"Get down, and stay still. There are lots of rabbits out here. The bread crumbs will attract them," he said, smiling.

Nearly five minutes passed.

"Look," Charlotte whispered. "There's one," she pointed toward a large bush.

Théo stepped forward. Threw once—missed—and threw again as the rabbit stumbled over an icy patch.

"Ah! *You* needed two knives, when I killed with one," she said, smiling.

"You think you are more expert with knives than I am?" Théo asked.

"*Mais bien sûr*. But of course," Charlotte said. Picking up a handful of snow, she shoved it in Théo's face, giggled, and ran.

"You'll lose this game." He grabbed her by the waist and threw her to the ground. Pouncing on top of her, he shoveled snow under her coat.

She let out a squeal—too loud for the quiet forest. He lay his gloved hand over her mouth and dropped down beside her. Slowly removing his hand, he pressed his lips against hers.

Breaking away, Charlotte touched his face. "I've come to love your kisses."

"And I've come to love you," Théo said, kissing her again.

***

They returned to the farmhouse to find Rémi gutting and cleaning a half-dozen rabbits in the sink.

The men had been busy hunting. "Meat for the stew, skins for the bed. Marie has a good start on a rabbit blanket. Once the pelts have dried she'll stitch them along the bottom of the blanket, forming a new row."

"I'll help with dinner as soon as I get changed. Got a little wet out there," Charlotte said, winking at Théo.

Once in the room, Charlotte pulled her coat and blouse off and looked down at her waist. A red and blistered rash encircled her body, just under the muslin bag that held the necklace. Removing the bag, Charlotte pressed on the rash. "Ouch!" Why hadn't she done something about it sooner? The diamonds had worn through the bag and rubbed her flesh raw. All for the diamonds, she thought. Why couldn't Father have kept them?

Théo knocked on the door and stepped inside.

Charlotte gasped, and turned to the wall.

"What happened? I didn't cause that, did I?" Théo said.

"No," she said, pulling on her blouse.

"Is that a necklace?" He asked, looking down at the bed. "Where'd it come from?"

"It's my family's necklace."

"Why do you have it?"

She handed it to him. He turned the diamonds in his hands, and whistled. "They're beautiful. But why didn't you tell us about them? If the Nazis learn you have something this precious, they'll raise the reward on the wanted posters—search harder for you, and that puts all of us at risk."

"But how could they know about it?"

"Your parents. Your aunt and uncle who were tortured by the Gestapo."

"It's my family's heirloom. My father insisted I take it with me," she said, sighing. "No one in my family would ever lead the Germans to me, even under torture. *No* one."

She reached for the necklace. "But I need a safe place to hide it," she said, dropping the diamonds back into the worn bag. "I can't wear it around my waist any longer."

"First let's have Marie look at your rash. You don't want it to get infected. She has some salve. I'll get her," he said, moving toward the door. "But you need to know the *maquisards* won't like this. Despite what you say about your family, you've risked our lives. The Germans will be flushing out *Maquis* after the sabotage. Add this to the destruction of a train, and we'll be number one on their list." Théo shook his head and left the room.

Charlotte sat down on the bed and sighed deeply. Tucking the necklace under the covers she wondered what Rémi would say? Would he send her away, now, just when she'd become part of the *maquisards*?

"So what is this I hear about a rash?" Marie asked, entering the room.

"It's all around my middle. The worst spot is right here." Charlotte said, pointing. "It's very raw."

"Let me look," Marie said.

She touched the rash, working her way around

Charlotte's waist.

"Pressing it hurts," Charlotte complained.

"It should," Marie said. "It's very red. I was testing for infection. I'll wash it and then apply the salve. You shouldn't have let it go so long."

Marie walked to the door. "I'll be back in a minute with medicine and bandages."

Why hadn't Marie asked about the necklace? Théo must have told her. He'd been so brusque.

Marie entered the room along with Théo. He carried a tall stool and set it down, then glanced at Charlotte. She frowned.

Théo helped her up on the stool and stood ready to help. With the added height, Marie could work around Charlotte more easily. She began washing the rash with soap and warm water.

"Don't be angry with Théo," Marie said, glancing over at him. "We're all in danger if the Germans learn about the necklace. Tell us about it. Why do you have it? Where did it come from?"

Marie applied the salve—rubbing it in. "Ow! My skin is really sore, and that medicine stings. It smells horrid, too!" Charlotte said.

"I'm sorry," Marie said. "I'll be more gentle, but I can't do anything about the smell."

"*Merci*," Charlotte replied, her eyes tearing. "About the necklace. It has been in our family for more than a century. It's a legend. The stones were cut from the famous French Blue, a diamond purchased by Louis XIV. His jeweler created a beautiful brooch for the king. But in the process, many carats were cut away—large and small diamonds. The king hid them in an ermine bag behind a credenza in his palace at Versailles."

"I've heard of the French Blue," Marie said. "Every school child knows the story. But these diamonds are a mystery to me. How did you come by them?" Marie asked.

"A diamond dealer from Torino purchased them in London during the French Revolution. He brought them to Italy and sold them to our family. They were recut and strung into a necklace. My family, the Settevendemies, lost most of our wealth during the years of Italian unification and the Great War, but we never sold the necklace."

"Why didn't your parents keep it in Italy? They put you in terrible danger," Marie said.

"My mother and father feared for my safety *and* the safety of the diamonds. Before I left Torino, Mother tied them around my waist, inside the muslin case. My father plans to sell some after the war to rebuild our home and vineyards. He felt they'd be more secure with me. I can't explain his logic. It wasn't my place to ask."

"We'll have to tell the others," Marie said. "The necklace must be hidden. Where, I don't know. But I'm curious. May I see it?"

"*Oui*, of course. It's tucked in my bedcovers."

Marie pulled it out. "*Mon Dieu!* It's—spectacular." She touched it as though the diamonds might shatter, like ice. "I've never seen such a brilliant blue." Marie held it up to her neck. "Too beautiful for me, I'm afraid," she said, smiling.

"The diamonds have a secret," Charlotte said, eager to share their story. "It helps to identify them. If you hold them in the sunlight, they turn orange. Bring them back inside, in a dark room, and they glow—slowly returning to their brilliant blue. I can show you later."

"Sounds like magic."

Charlotte smiled and nodded. "It is."

***

That evening, Charlotte retold the story of the diamonds and how her family came to own them. When she finished, she held up the necklace. The *maquisards* insisted on inspecting it—holding it to the light. The diamonds sparkled a radiant blue.

"We need a secure hiding place for the necklace," Rémi said. "It's too dangerous for Charlotte to carry, and we can't hide it in the farmhouse. The banks are out of the question. The *Boches* manage them."

"Why not bury it, just beyond our house?" Jules asked.

"Or perhaps in the quarry," Patrick said.

"I know where it will be safe—the *Maquis* cave on Cap Ferrat," Robin offered.

"Of course," Théo murmured. "The Germans will never find it there. I can take Charlotte tomorrow. We'll travel at dusk, stay overnight, and return the next day."

"First, tell me more about the cave," Charlotte said. "Is it safe? How many people know about it?"

"Very few," Rémi said. "But I can't let you risk

your life or endanger one of our men for a necklace—no matter how precious."

"You're as bad as the Gestapo," Charlotte said hastily, a headache setting in. "You want me to choose between my family and the *Maquis*. Don't put me in that position. It isn't fair."

"I'll take her to the cave," Théo said. "Charlotte's right. We can't ask her to decide between us and her family. Would you ask me to betray the *Maquis*?"

"Of course not," Rémi said, rubbing his chin.

Charlotte frowned and hung her head. "I don't want any of you to risk your lives for the necklace, and I don't want you to be angry with me or with each other."

Rémi nodded.

She scanned the faces of the men. "Tell me where the cave is. I'll go by myself."

"I understand your concern—for us and for your family," Rémi said. "The cave is too well hidden. You'd never find it on your own. Théo can take you."

She sighed—worried.

"But understand," Rémi cautioned again, "this is *very* dangerous."

Chapter 19
The *Maquis* Cave
Cap Ferrat

Dusk—a dangerous time to slip unnoticed through the streets of Old Nice. Curfew was in place. Germans patrolled.

Charlotte felt Théo take her hand.

"The Cap Ferrat footpath is on the other side of the ancient Château, which is just above us."

Charlotte nodded.

"Hurry while there's still light."

East of Nice they came to the peninsula of Cap Ferrat and beyond that the village of Beaulieu-sur-mer.

"I've never seen Germans on the east side of the peninsula or on the footpath that leads to the *Maquis* cave. I think the *Boches* are too lazy to walk," Théo said. "But keep an eye open for them, just in case."

Théo led Charlotte across railroad tracks to the trailhead of a stone path, just above the water's edge. "Point St-Hospice is at the tip of the peninsula. The *chapelle* is there too. Follow me."

"You're very familiar with this area," Charlotte said.

"*Oui*. This was my summer playground. I spent hours here during the summer with Rémi—swimming and playing."

It grew colder as they walked. An icy wind blew off the wine-dark sea. Charlotte rubbed her hands together. The stones were slick—washed by sea spray. She slipped, then righted herself.

Taking her mind off the bitter winds, she thought of the summers she'd played with Rémi, collecting rocks and shells. Flowers were in bloom, a lavender scented breeze drifted over them, and the water was a brilliant blue. That was not so long ago. But their world had changed forever.

"Théo," she whispered. "Wait. I need to button my coat. I'm freezing." She paused and secured her coat.

He stopped, and stood besider her, silently.

Voices came with a gust of wind. Just above them. Heavy soles crunched on pebbles.

"Down," Théo hissed. Crouching against the sea wall, he pulled her to his chest. Charlotte felt his heart pounding—hard and fast.

"*Halt*. I heard something," a man said in German.

"*Nur Wind*," said another. "Your imagination. Only wind and waves."

Charlotte's breath came in shallow gasps. What would happen if they were caught? Rémi was right. The danger was real. She pressed hard against Théo.

Glancing back at the trail, she saw her glove. She'd dropped it when buttoning her coat! Small and gray—perhaps the soldiers would miss it.

"Charlotte," Théo whispered. "Get your knife." She nodded.

They waited and listened. Charlotte heard the men draw closer to the overhang. They must be scanning the trail. Below, a wave dashed against the rocks and washed over the walkway. The glove, gone with a retreating wave. Relief flooded through her.

"It's bitter. Our patrol is up. Time to go," the soldier said.

"They said they're leaving," Charlotte whispered.

"Don't move," Théo murmured. "It could be a ruse."

Minutes passed. They heard nothing.

"Okay, let's go," Théo said. Stiff and chilled, Charlotte rose and followed him.

A dim light shone ahead. She tugged on Théo's coat. "What's that?" she whispered.

"It's Chapelle St-Hospice. The hospital is just above us, surrounded by trees."

As they rounded the corner, a figure walked toward them. Too late to turn around, or hide.

"*Halt!* It's past curfew. Who are you, and why are you here?" The German soldier clicked his flashlight on, and moved the beam across their faces. "Show me your papers!"

They dug in their pockets, stalling. Charlotte, thinking of the wanted poster and the sketch—fuzzy and dated, but possibly enough to identify her.

Be quick, Charlotte cautioned herself. Think up a story. Engage him in idle talk. Anything to keep our papers out of his hands.

"I've come from Chapelle St-Hospice," she said. "My mother is very ill. I pray for her recovery."

"Praying won't help. You're better off asking favors from the Führer," the German snorted. The soldier peered at her. "Your German is good, but you have a French accent. Do you live here?"

"My father was German, my mother French," Charlotte lied.

"Why aren't you in Germany?" the soldier asked.

She reached for her St-Anne medal, rubbing it for strength. "Father was badly wounded during the Great War. Mother told me he was never right again."

"Never right? What do you mean? Germans are not weak."

"I don't know. I was very young. Didn't understand. Then, one day he hanged himself."

"He was not a true German," the soldier said, spitting on the ground.

Charlotte ignored the remark. "Mother discovered him in the barn. After that, she cried often and coughed constantly. Maybe she had TB. Grandmother wrote and pleaded with us to return to France. Said she would care for us, and she has." The charade was hard to maintain. Charlotte hoped the German would let them go, soon.

"You should have stayed in Germany," the soldier said. "You have the blond hair of an Aryan and you're attractive. You'd make a good wife and mother strong German children—even though you have French blood. Your children would have less."

Charlotte blanched. "My mother is very sick. She gets weaker by the day. I think she is dying."

"The strong survive," the German said. "And who is this man?" the soldier pointed at Théo. "Is he mute?"

"He's kind enough to walk me to the chapel and home again. A friend of my grandmother. He only speaks French."

He waved his hand in dismissal. "Go back to your grandmother. If you must pray, do it during the day. And *do not* ignore curfew. If I see you again, I'll have you both arrested. Understand?"

"*Danke. Gute Nacht.*" Charlotte said, offering a slight curtsy.

Charlotte slipped her arm through Théo's, and the couple hurried up the path.

"Bastard," Théo whispered.

At the top of the trail, they left the stone walkway and stepped onto a dirt path.

"We've gone slightly past the cave entrance, but not far," Théo said. "We should stop and listen before moving on. The *Boche* may have followed us." He took her hand. "Come up here, behind the boulders."

The southerly wind blew hard. Sounds of thrashing trees and pounding surf filled the air. Charlotte shook. Théo pulled her close, holding her tightly.

Minutes passed. Maybe ten.

Théo whispered, "Follow me. If we can't hear the

Boche, he can't hear us. Stay low."

The shore was rocky and pockmarked. Dry lichen crackled underfoot and the water lapped inches from their feet. The wind, sharp and biting.

"We're close," Théo said. "I need to find the cairns that mark the entrance. I don't dare use my flashlight." She could barely see him as he worked his way from stone to stone, searching for the cairns.

Had she done the right thing—coming to the cave? Perhaps it *was* a stupid notion. Their lives were more important than a necklace. Maybe she should have listened to Patrick. "Bury it in the forest," he'd said. "Keep it a secret. It will be there after the war— probably."

Théo whispered, "I found it."

She worked her way toward his voice. He'd opened a hidden door—a small dark opening to the cave. Théo pulled her in.

He reached back and pulled the trap-door closed, latching it.

Théo took a deep breath and let it out slowly. "We're safe."

Charlotte clicked on her flashlight. Théo was ghostly pale. Her own face must look the same.

Shining her light around the interior, she realized it was not a true cave, but carved out of the hillside and lined with rocks. Stones covered the floor, elevating it above the sea. Damp and dark, the air smelled of the sea. It felt like a tomb.

"Someone worked a long time to build this

hideaway," Charlotte said.

"*Oui*." Théo swept his light over the walls. "This was once a very small grotto. Rémi's grandfather dug into the seawall and lined it with stones, then secured the entrance with more stones and a small hatch-like door. He made it soon after he immigrated from Russia. He wanted a place to hide his family—just in case. Now we use it to hide from our enemy, just as Rémi's grandfather feared." He shook his head.

"It's well stocked," Charlotte said, flashing her light on shelves that lined the cave.

"Mattresses, blankets, food, and water." Théo said. "When the Germans occupied northern France, Rémi and I brought more provisions. Some canned meats. Lots of pasta and rice. Nuts. Not a balanced diet, but it would keep us alive while we continued to work."

Charlotte felt a touch of cool air on her neck. "Is there a vent?" she asked, glancing around.

"Yes. A small one extends upwards to the boulders, where we hid earlier. That limits mold, and assures fresh air for a dozen or so people at one time."

Théo wrapped his arms around Charlotte. "Enough about the cave."

She welcomed his touch. They could just as easily be in front of a firing squad, or tortured by the Gestapo. But they were here, safe—for now.

"Tell me," he said, smiling, "how did you come up with that story about your mother and father? If you hadn't been so quick...."

She laughed. "Pietro and I used to make up stories

all the time. A game we played—trying to fool the other. Sometimes we succeeded. Innocent children. Innocent times."

"I think your brother just saved our lives."

"Perhaps he is our guardian angel," she said, smiling.

Théo drew her close again. She heard him sigh. Then his lips were on hers. She moaned, tightening her hold. A few more kisses and Théo pulled away with a last soft breath on her cheek. "We should hide your necklace, then I'll make some tea—warm us up."

"Where is the best place to hide it?" she asked.

Théo flashed the light around the floor and walls of the cave. "We can see most of the interior from here. Shine your light up there," he pointed, "where the wall and ceiling meet."

Charlotte saw a reddish stone, slightly recessed from the others. "That looks like a good place."

"We can pull the stone out and put the necklace behind it. When the rock is back in place, it won't stand out. Hold the light, I'll pry it loose."

He wrapped a bit of fabric over the metal tip of his knife. "This'll keep the blade from scoring the surrounding rocks and giving the hiding place away."

He wedged the knife between the stones and popped the red one out. "Hold it while I dig a little deeper."

Dirt and sand scattered on the floor as Théo carved. He turned to Charlotte. "Are you ready to let the cave guard your necklace?"

"Yes, but let me put it in the hollow," she said, hands shaking.

"*Certainement*. Can you reach?"

"Not quite."

He lifted her up. She kissed the necklace good-bye and placed it in the wall.

Théo set her down. She felt anxious. This was her father's fortune. He'd given it to her for safekeeping. Maybe she hadn't done the right thing, letting it out of her hands. And what of Théo? Could he be trusted to keep her secret?

Théo whispered in her ear, "Don't worry. Your necklace will be safe. You'll come back, take it home, and plant your vines."

"Pray," she sighed, "pray that my parents are safe. Sometimes I think I should return to Italy, but the Germans would find and kill me. I'm certain."

"Your father was right to send you to France. Don't worry. You're here. Hand me the red stone, and I'll put it back in place."

"Perfect," she said, taking in a deep breath and blowing it out slowly. But doubt plagued her. What if both she and Théo were killed in the war? The necklace would be lost forever and her parents—paupers.

"Promise to keep this a secret," she said, a quaver in her voice.

"It's our secret." Taking her by the hand, he walked over to the shelves.

"Let's pull a couple of mattresses down. They'll insulate us from the stones on the floor. Grab a couple of blankets, too."

Théo set the mattresses side by side, and spread a blanket over them.

"Sit here and I'll heat the water, and light some candles," he said.

Charlotte knew she was naïve. Her parents had protected her. Lorenzo was her only suitor, and they'd rejected him. She understood that she and Théo would sleep next to each other—under one blanket, but what else? Would he make love to her? Did she want him to? Was he the man she'd spend a lifetime with? He'd told the others about her necklace, but now he was risking his life to hide it. Surely he was committed to her.

Charlotte played nervously with her glove.

Théo placed the candles on the stones, lit them, and draped a small blanket over her shoulders.

"The water is boiling. *Café crème, mademoiselle?*" he teased.

"*Thê nature, merci,*" she said, taking the cup. "If only it *were* coffee and not tea!"

"When the war is over, we'll drink *café crème* together, and much more," he said.

She smiled, warming her hands on the sides of the mug.

He sat next to her as they sipped the hot tea.

"Théo, I've seen a different French flag, from time to time, and there is one right there," she pointed to the flag draped from a shelf. "Why is there a Cross of Lorraine in the white section?"

"Ah," Théo said, "it is our Resistance flag. General

de Gaulle wanted something different from the old tri-color. It's used by Vichy France—those that sold out to the Germans. The Cross of Lorraine was once carried by Joan of Arc—on a banner. De Gaulle had the image sewn on the old tri-color to give us courage and to defend our nation against the ugly swastika. The Free French army use the flag, as does the Resistance in the cities, and the Maquis in the countryside. You don't see it too often, though."

"And why is that?"

"It announces who we are, and we want to stay hidden. But many people hang them in their homes. There is one in Rémi's room. I think he likes to wake up to the sight of the flag. It gives him courage, or so he says."

"I like the story. Someday I'd like a flag of my own," she said.

Theo grinned. "But ... and tomorrow. We'll leave very early—before dawn. We should blend in with others on their way to market."

"I'll be ready," she said.

"You look tired. We need to spread a few more blankets, but if you get cold in the night ... um, I can hold you."

Charlotte blushed, finished her tea, and handed him the cup.

They took more blankets from the shelves and spread them over the mattress. Slipping off her skirt, she lifted the linen bandage.

Théo glanced at it. "That looks much better."

"It doesn't sting anymore," she said, smiling.

"You're shaking. You must be cold. Slide into bed and I'll snuff the candles."

As she moved under the covers, she realized two things—she loved Théo, and the war had changed everything. Life was short. There may be no tomorrow.

Théo moved closer. "I'll warm you."

They held each other for a moment, then Charlotte felt Théo's soft kisses on her neck. She giggled and snuggled closer, warming to his touch.

His lips on hers, then a tongue soft and moist. She groaned, longing for his touch, but anxious.

"Théo," she whispered.

"*Oui?*"

"I've never made love before. I know very little. Mother said she'd tell me on my wedding eve."

"Do you want me to make love to you?" he asked.

"*Oui*," she whispered. "I do love you." He filled her with a heat she'd never known. Charlotte wondered: would this moment ever come again? Could this be their last chance to make love? "And if we should live through this war...."

"We *will* live," Théo said. "Never lose faith."

Théo kissed her, and moved his hand under her blouse. "Are you ready?" he asked, stroking her breasts, tenderly.

"Will it hurt?" she said, breathlessly.

"Only a little. The first time. You should be okay."

She nodded.

He seemed eager, but his touch—inviting. Stop

worrying, she chided herself, and began to move as her body demanded, in a soft, slow rhythm, abandoning her reservations.

Tears of passion filled her eyes. "I *do* love you. Your touch tells me...."

"Hush. We will be together, always," Théo said.

"*Oui, toujours*," Charlotte sighed.

Chapter 20
Lysander Down
Tourrettes-sur-Loup

"You're back," Rémi said as Théo and Charlotte entered the farmhouse. "Good. I've been working the wireless, outdoors with Robin. There's lots to share."

"What happened?" Théo asked.

Marie hugged Charlotte and Théo. "Rémi's been up all night."

"I'll fill you in," he said, rubbing his hands in front of the fire.

"Are the men safe?" Charlotte asked.

"Yes. But a British pilot crash-landed last night near Tourrettes-sur-Loup." Rémi shook his head imagining the pilot's desperate landing. "He was way off course. Ground fog was thick, and he missed signals. Landed in a small pasture—gliding in on an empty tank."

"*Mon Dieu*," said Théo. "It's very mountainous there. Was he hurt?"

"His leg is badly broken. A family in Tourrettes took him in, but he needs a doctor to set the leg, and the *Boches* are patrolling the area."

"What can we do?" Charlotte asked, leaning toward the hearth.

"The *maquisards* in Cannes would normally take this on. It's their territory. But their leader, Margarite, was taken prisoner by the *Malice*—the French Gestapo. The *Maquis* are trying to get her out of prison—but there are only two of them and they're also monitoring news from the Allies. So, they've asked us to help.

"Robin is trying to contact a *maquisard* in Grasse. No luck yet. The men in Tourrettes are eager to help, but they don't have a truck. They'll need one to deliver the Brit to the hospital in Grasse. Right now they're out camouflaging the plane. If the Germans find it, they'll do a house-to-house search for the pilot. Innocent people will die."

Rémi sat down in one of the nearby chairs. He rubbed his forehead and eyes. His head throbbed. "I hope to God this war ends soon," he mumbled.

Marie moved next to him, and began rubbing his back and neck. He placed a hand on hers.

"One good thing," Rémi added with a sigh. "The plane was full of guns and ammunition. The villagers have hidden the cache. We'll have it when the Allies invade."

"Did the pilot bring an SOE?" Charlotte asked. "Churchill wants his Special Operations Executives in France. I've heard they're often flown in on Lysanders."

"Only supplies this time," Rémi said.

Théo moved closer to Rémi. "What's the plan?"

"You'll join me," Rémi said, glancing at Théo. "Just the two of us. We'll pick up the pilot and transport him to Grasse."

"Let me help," Charlotte said.

Rémi heard the urgency in her voice.

"I can steady the pilot—comfort him in the truck," she said.

"I need you here with the rest of the team. We've heard the Nazis are planning an attack on Falicon, because of the train sabotage. No surprise, but we must relocate—immediately."

"Where to?" Jules asked.

"Vence. There are *Maquis* in the village. Two. I know them both. They're searching for an empty farmhouse. They should have one by tomorrow.

"We'll all leave together, before dawn. I'll drop you off in Vence with the *maquisards*. Théo and I will drive on to Tourrettes and pick up the Englishman.

"Robin, destroy all of our communication, documents, wireless notes, anything that might lead the Gestapo to our families or incriminate *Maquis* cells along the Riviera. The rest of you, pack sparingly.

"Any more questions?" Rémi asked, exhaustion lacing his voice.

Charlotte glanced at Théo, then back at Rémi. "Is this a very dangerous mission?"

"Yes," Rémi said. He heard worry in her voice that hadn't been there before. She and Théo were lovers, now. A night in the *Maquis* cave. He'd expected no less. But he couldn't let their passion compromise the mission.

Rémi stood and gave Charlotte a hug. "Don't worry. We'll return by tomorrow evening." He kissed her on the forehead and gave her hand a quick squeeze.

Turning back to the *Maquis*, he said, "Alright. Let's get started. Théo and I'll prepare the truck. The rest of you—pack.

"Oh, one more thing. Marie, I'll need you to paint 'plumber' on the side of the truck," Remi said.

"I'll work with Charlotte on that," Marie said.

Worry etched Charlotte's face.

"I've learned," Marie said, taking Charlotte's hand, "the only way to push the fear away is to keep moving, keep busy. Come, we'll start on the truck ... then pack."

"This is hard on the team," Rémi said to Théo.

Charlotte turned, but not before she heard Théo respond. "If you're referring to the women, they're just as strong as we are. You should have heard Charlotte last night when a German guard detained us. We're both here today because of her."

Rémi nodded. But no matter how daring Marie and Charlotte were, he worried about them more than the others. They were women, after all, and if the Gestapo got hold of them ....

"I'll gather blankets and a board to splint the Brit's leg," Rémi said. "I want explosives, too. Do we have fuses and plastique?"

"*Oui,*" Théo said.

"We may need to blow up the road," Rémi said, "if we're spotted and Germans give chase."

Chapter 21
Greeks Bearing Gifts
Grasse

Rémi drove through the morning darkness, Théo beside him. The Falicon *Maquis* hunkered in the back of the truck. They arrived in Vence shortly after sunrise.

The local *maquisards* waited at the agreed upon place. Stepping out of the truck, Rémi said, "Théo and I will return soon. Perhaps tonight—certainly tomorrow."

"We'll have your unit settled in a safe house by then," the Vence *maquisard* said. "*Bonne chance, mon ami.*"

Rémi took Marie in his arms. He felt her anxiety—her shoulders stiffened.

"Don't worry," he said. "We'll be back soon."

"But I do worry," she said, tracing his jaw with her finger. "You're tense and tired. I feel it."

Rémi let Marie go and stood back, waiting.

Théo kissed Charlotte. "Never forget what I said. *Toujours.*"

"Théo...," Charlotte whispered.

"They'll be back soon. You must have faith," Marie reassured her.

"It's time," Rémi said to Théo. The two men jumped back into the truck, and set out for Tourrettes.

"Watch for road blocks," Rémi said. "The street is filled with hairpin turns. You might be able to spot the *Boches* before they see us."

"Looks good so far," Théo said.

They drove for an hour without saying a word. Their guns in their laps, cocked and ready to use.

Rémi broke the silence. "I didn't want to say this earlier, but there may be a collaborator in our midst. Perhaps in Tourrettes."

"Who told you that?" Théo asked.

"Robin picked it up on the wireless—last night."

Théo took in a deep breath, and blew it out slowly. "God help us."

***

Before noon, Rémi and Théo spotted the village of Tourrettes-sur-Loup, just over a small valley. Rémi clutched the steering wheel, trying to navigate the narrow serpentine road. As they neared the village, the road dipped down past a boarded-up candy factory, then over a bridge spanning a small river.

"Turn to the right and park by the waterfall, out of sight of the road. Who's your contact?" Théo asked.

"His name is Jean. He owns the Café Diana," Rémi said. He parked and stepped out of the truck. "Wait here."

Rémi hurried up the sidewalk in search of the café.

Jean waited at the door. "Come in, *mon ami*." He tipped his head toward a corner table. "We can talk over there. Can I get you something to eat?"

"*Un café, s'il vous plaît. Merci.* That is all."

Jean signaled the bar. Keeping his voice low he said, "We finally heard from the *maquisard* in Grasse. I think your fellow, Robin, was trying to contact him. He goes by the name of Bernard. He assured me there's a doctor at the hospital who'll treat the Englishman."

After the coffee was served Jean leaned forward and whispered, "Go to the only café in Grasse. It's on the main street, just beyond the statue of *Comte de Grasse*. The front door is a weathered yellow. Ask for André. If the waiter feigns ignorance, ask for Annette. If he says he'll check with the owner—run. The site's been compromised."

Rémi swallowed hard. "We need to do this. It's the decent thing. We owe it to the British."

"You know the Gestapo prison is there. The only good thing about Grasse is the hospital. The Englishman will be lucky to keep his leg. If it has to be amputated, it must be done there."

"Alright. Let's get him into the truck. The sooner Théo and I are on the road the better."

Jean nodded.

As Rémi neared the truck he spotted Théo leaning against the vehicle, smoking a cigarette and looking impatient.

"You were gone a long time. What did you learn?"

Théo asked.

"The *Boches* are everywhere. Here comes Jean. Stay here. Jean and I'll get the Brit. His name is Giles."

"I may smoke my weekly ration before you return," Théo said.

"A young barmaid will bring you some coffee. If she stays to chat, be careful what you say," Rémi added.

Within twenty minutes Rémi and Jean returned with the pilot. They supported him as he hopped on one leg, groaning with each step. His pant leg was rolled up, revealing a blood-soaked white cotton bandage—bone pressing against the wrap. The leg bent in an unnatural way. Bruises and deep scrapes covered the man's body.

Théo winced, and drew in a sharp breath.

Jean and Théo helped Rémi lift Giles into the truck. The Brit was as white as freshly bleached sheets. Shock had set in.

"Here's a blanket," Rémi said, dropping it over the pilot. "It gets cold back here."

The Brit nodded and groaned, "Thank you."

Jean handed him a small bottle of brandy. "For the pain."

***

By midafternoon they'd reached the outskirts of Grasse, a village set against the side of a mountain. As they approached the Hotel de Ville, Rémi saw a city caught in the grip of war. No sign of life. Shops boarded, windows broken, stuccoed walls peeling and crumbling. Weeds pushing the flowers away. Once a spa for Europeans seeking quiet and relaxation, it now hosted the Gestapo prison for the hill towns of Provence.

Rémi pulled into a side street and cut the motor. The café was only a few blocks away.

"Have we made a terrible mistake?" Théo asked. "The village looks dead. Is the hospital still functioning? Could this be a trap?"

Rémi gripped the steering wheel and lay his head against it—exhaustion and tension taking their toll. He sat up slowly. "Jean says the hospital is open. Confirmed by the Grasse *maquisard*. Instructions are to meet our contact in the café. He'll escort us to the hospital and connect us with the doctor."

Grabbing his pistol, he tucked it into his holster, and opened the door. Looking back at Théo, he said, "If our contact isn't in the café, we'll abandon Grasse and head north to St-Vallier."

Rémi set out for the café. With only a few shops open, it wasn't difficult to find. He opened the door and entered a small dark room. It smelled of wine, smoke, and men who'd long ago given up bathing. Heads turned as Rémi walked to the counter. Four grizzled men sat at a small square table, sipping *pastis,* muttering among themselves.

"I'm looking for André," Rémi said to the waiter. "Does he work on Tuesday?"

"Sorry, *monsieur*, there's no one here by that name. I would suggest another café, but this is the only one open."

Rémi took a deep breath, "And Annette, is she

here?"

Glancing over Rémi's shoulder, the waiter shook his head.

Either the password was wrong, thought Rémi, or I've just let the Gestapo know I'm in Grasse.

"Perhaps I'm in the wrong village," Rémi said, stepping toward the door. "I travel without a map."

As Rémi left the café, he glanced at the small table where the four men had been seated. Only three remained.

Before stepping off the curb, he looked up and down the road. That's when he saw them. Gestapo. Five of them walked east, in the shadow of the buildings, their backs to him.

Rémi slipped behind a building, peering out to confirm their path. The man in the café was in the lead. They were headed toward the truck.

Rémi's mouth went dry. *"Mon Dieu,"* he whispered. *"We're trapped."*

When the Gestapo turned south, Rémi circled quickly on side streets until he got back to the street the truck was parked on. He was three blocks up the hill. Edging forward, he looked around the corner.

Someone had sent the Gestapo right to their truck.

Five German soldiers surrounded the vehicle. Four more armed men waited at each street corner. Théo stood, hands overhead and pressed against the nearby building, a gun to his temple. Two soldiers peered into the back of the truck where the Englishman lay. Another soldier searched the cab.

The plastique! Rémi remembered. *Putain!*

He scanned the nearby streets again. The Gestapo were waiting for him, he was certain. The Grasse *maquisard*—the collaborator.

A pitiful scream filled the air! So intense, it tore through Rémi's head.

The *Boches* were pulling the Englishman out of the truck—by his broken leg. They threw Giles on the ground. A German hit him in the head with the butt of his rifle. The pilot went silent.

"Have mercy on us," mumbled Rémi, backing away from the corner. He leaned against the building, wiping his damp palms on his shirt. Taking a deep breath, he peered out again. The Englishman hadn't moved, nor had Théo—still against the wall.

But one thing *had* changed. There were more soldiers than before and they were spreading out, in all four directions. A manhunt was on, and Rémi was the target.

He had two choices: stay and kill as many Germans as possible before they killed him, or run. If he ran, there was a chance he'd escape and return to rescue Théo and the Brit. The choice was easy.

Run.

Chapter 22
Then There Was One
Grasse

Rémi darted between buildings, keeping an eye out for Gestapo. An alarm wailed in the distance, putting the city on alert. The *Boches* must want him badly.

When he reached the outskirts of Grasse, Rémi had a choice—go around the mountain that backed up against the village, or climb over it. He suspected the Gestapo would watch both routes, but he'd take the most difficult. They'd have to work harder to find him.

He began climbing—stopping often to listen for anyone who might be in pursuit.

The mountain was steep, craggy, and full of outcroppings and dry underbrush. The small, water-starved trees provided little cover. No path or trail. He kept low to the ground, slipping often but steadying himself by grasping large rocks and clumps of tall dry *maquis.*

Three hours passed before Rémi reached the top.

By the time he scrambled to the crest, the sun had set. Stopping to catch his breath, he turned and scanned below.

Headlights moved through the village streets. Flashlights bobbed along the base of the mountain.

Scudding clouds intermittently blocked a full moon—just enough light for Rémi to see a rough trail down the backside of the mountain. Descending, he hoped he wouldn't meet Germans climbing up.

"God help me," he whispered, "and God help Théo."

It took two hours to work his way down. Peering through the dim light, he could make out a road about a hundred meters below. Was this the same road he'd driven yesterday? Exhaustion clouded his memory. He tried to picture the road map. Turn left to St-Valliére-de-Thiey. Turn right to Vence.

A well-worn path ran parallel to the road, meandering through thick clumps of shrubs and shade trees. It would be difficult for anyone to see him from the street.

A branch cracked behind him! Rémi reached for his gun, only to see a deer jump to the side of the trail, skirt him, and run through the brush. He walked on, but lack of sleep and a night of stumbling through thickets left him exhausted. Dizzy and nauseated, he needed a safe place to sleep—if only for a few hours.

On his right, dense bushes encircled a copse of trees. Trying to leave the undergrowth undisturbed, he scrambled into the brush, curled up, and slept.

Four hours later, just before daylight, he woke groggy and famished. Rémi rubbed his stubbled face, again wondering how the Gestapo had trapped them. Who was Bernard? How were the Germans able to access the *Maquis* wireless? Until he had answers, none of his men would be safe, and rescuing Théo— impossible.

Just as the sun rose, Rémi spotted a farmhouse. He stopped and asked for bread and water. "Please stay," the family encouraged him. "You can sleep in the loft."

He thanked them, accepted a packet of food, and quickly moved on.

✳✳✳

For three long days, Rémi walked back roads and trails. He stopped often to ask for food and water, but never stayed more than a few minutes. He skirted Tourrettes—determined not to put the villagers or himself at risk. He focused his thoughts on one goal— free Théo and the pilot.

Rémi arrived in Vence at sunrise on the fourth day. He immediately sought out one of the village *maquisards*. Bruno lived in a small cottage on the edge of town. Rémi knocked on his friend's door. Bruno opened up, and Rémi stumbled inside. Finally feeling safe, he let his exhaustion overcome him, and collapsed.

Bruno lifted Rémi and helped him into a chair. He made tea and served him a cup mixed with brandy. "Take this. It'll warm you."

Rémi's hands shook as he accepted the cup. He blew on the liquid to cool it, sipped, and sighed deeply.

"The hill towns are thick with roadblocks and German soldiers. Gestapo are everywhere. How did you avoid them?" Bruno asked.

Rémi took a second sip and closed his eyes. "Not easy. I saw them, but they never spotted me. Have the Gestapo been in Vence?"

"Yes. They search the streets day and night. After dark, they'd shine a bright light in the windows and around the houses. They haven't bothered me—yet. I've never seen such a man hunt."

Rémi nodded.

"We heard rumors of your escape. Théo and the Brit—captured. Tell me what happened."

"First," Rémi said, leaning back in the chair, "did you find a house for the Falicon *Maquis*?"

"They're in a farmhouse on the outskirts of the village—the other side of town. They're as safe as we can make them."

"Grasse was a trap," Rémi said. "We walked right into it. Someone betrayed us."

"Shortly after you left," Bruno said, "we discovered the wireless code had been compromised. A German in Grasse posed as a *maquisard*. We had no way to warn you."

Rémi groaned.

"The Gestapo will not give up until they capture you. If they can't immediately find you, they'll spread stories of Théo's torture, hoping to flush you out. They may even post photographs. They'll provoke you to do something risky. Then they'll have you both."

"Tell me how the wireless was compromised," Rémi asked.

"Perhaps someone in Tourrettes collaborated with the Germans," Bruno said, shrugging. "We've abandoned the radio until we know who the traitor is and we have a new code. For now, we only communicate with handwritten messages, left in drop-off sites. Your *Maquis* are actively engaged. That's how we knew you were still alive, and Théo captured."

"Take me to the farmhouse," Rémi said.

"First, you must rest. I'll send a message that you're here, and safe."

Rémi nodded. Putting his cup down, he leaned back in the chair, closed his eyes, and slept.

Chapter 23
Falicon *Maquis*
Vence, France

"There must be something we can do," Charlotte said. "We know Rémi is making his way toward Vence. Messages confirm it. Why can't we go get him? Design a plan to rescue Théo? Every hour we do nothing...." She shook her head. Knowing Théo was a prisoner made her sick with fear.

"If we search for Rémi, the Gestapo are sure to spot us. We'll lead them right to him. Then they have us all," Robin said.

Charlotte tore at a hangnail. The pain was nothing compared to what Théo must be suffering. They knew he'd been moved from the prison in Grasse to Gestapo headquarters in Nice. She let her mind drift to that special night in the *Maquis* cave, and wondered if they would ever know each other again as they had that night, as man and wife.

"I don't think we can wait for Rémi," Charlotte

said. "The Gestapo may capture him too. Then we've lost precious time. If we don't free Théo in the next forty-eight hours, he could be dead by the time we get there."

"We must wait," Marie said. "If we're lucky...."

A knock at the door.

Patrick held his finger to his lips.

"It's Bruno," a voice from outside said. "I have Rémi."

Jules peeked through the curtain, and nodded to the *maquisards*. "Open the door. Rémi's back!" Charlotte's heart soared—surely Rémi would want to rescue Théo.

Marie fell into Rémi's arms the second he entered the farmhouse. He stumbled backward, but she and Patrick held him up and found him a chair.

"Get the man some food," Jules said. "No more hugging until he's eaten."

Quiet laughter filled the room. Charlotte joined in, but still worried about Théo.

"I'll prepare something," Marie said. "But talk loudly, so I can hear from the kitchen!"

Charlotte knelt in front of Rémi and took his hands. "Théo was taken to Nice. The Gestapo headquarters. After you rest, we'll plan his rescue."

He cupped his hands around her face. "Don't think I abandoned Théo just to save myself."

"I would *never* think that!" Charlotte said.

Rémi glanced at the *maquisards*. "We were compromised from the start. No one was in the café in Grasse to meet us. We were set up. By the time I got back to the truck, Théo was surrounded by Gestapo. A German held a gun to his head."

Charlotte gasped and shuddered.

"If I'd attempted a rescue they'd have killed him instantly," Rémi said. "I promise you, we *will* free Théo."

Chapter 24
Gestapo Headquarters
Nice

Théo looked out through the bars of his cell. Small cage-like rooms lined the basement walls. There were other prisoners—maybe three or four—hard to tell in the dim light. Bars surrounded them all. The floors were concrete, with one large drain in the center of the room. It was bitter cold, and the smell of vomit, feces, and blood filled the air. This wasn't a prison, Théo guessed, it was a torture chamber.

"I know this building," Théo whispered to the Brit. Their cells touched. "It was a hotel before the war."

"I'm afraid," Giles said. "The infection.... Look at my leg."

Théo glanced down, then closed his eyes and looked away. The wound festered. Flesh around the edges was greenish white. Even if help came today, the Brit might not live.

"Pray the *Maquis* will come soon," Théo said.

Hoping his words would give the pilot comfort.

"If I don't survive," the Englishman continued, "tell my parents I died shortly after crashing, and I didn't suffer long. My name is Giles William Miller. Please remember."

"Don't give up," Théo pleaded.

"Quiet!" A guard yelled, raking his rifle across the bars. "No talking!"

Two days passed. No one questioned them. No one tortured them. They were given bread and water the first day, and only water on the second. Théo feared what was coming, but the guards weren't talking. Perhaps this was a subtle form of torture—not knowing.

Late on the second day, a guard bellowed, "The Hunter arrives tomorrow. Then the fun begins!"

Théo shuddered. He'd heard of The Hunter. Everyone had. Théo's chance of survival narrowed considerably. The Hunter was a known sadist. His techniques—brutal.

That night, Théo couldn't sleep. He tried to distract himself by thinking of Charlotte. She'd blossomed from a shy, insecure young woman into a brilliant *maquisard*. He must not fail her. He'd promised they would be together ... *toujours.*

***

Théo stood in the middle of the room, hands bound in front. He didn't feel well. No food in more than twenty-four hours. His clothes were filthy, and his hair disheveled. The Germans had taken his shoes. The cold seeped up his legs, cramping them.

Two guards waited in the shadows.

The Hunter stepped into the darkened basement. A single bare light illuminated an open space in the center of the room. Prisoners could watch through the bars as inmates were questioned, beaten, and tormented.

Smoke spiraled from a cigarette in The Hunter's right hand. His brown uniform—carefully tailored and pressed. He wore shoes with a slight lift, giving the impression he was taller than his short stature suggested. He stroked a small kitten curled in the crook of his left arm. Except for the shaved head, he was the epitome of a kind, well-schooled gentleman. The Hunter had only one rival— Klaus Barbie, the Butcher of Lyon.

Théo reached down to massage a calf. A battered chair, covered with bloodstains and deep gouges, was in front of him. The overhead light cast grim shadows.

The Hunter began his well-practiced questioning.

"Please, *Monsieur* Théo, or is it Hugo Girard?" The Hunter said, grinning. "Take a seat. There is no reason for you to stand. You must be tired, and your feet— cold. Tsk, tsk." He stroked the tiny kitten. It purred in his arms. Trusting.

Théo glared at The Hunter, but remained standing.

"Oh, we're defiant, are we? Let's see if I can tempt you to answer my questions. Would you like some bread? Oh, but *excusez-moi*, you would prefer *brioche*, *oui?* One of your queens suggested the masses eat *brioche*, did she not?"

"*Oui*, she did," Théo replied. "Soon afterwards she was guillotined. Is that my fate? If it is, do it now and finish with the charade."

"Oh, *mon ami*. Very good. You imagine this a game of charades? Let's see how well you play."

Théo tried to grin, but feared a weak smile was all that rippled across his lips.

"So, my happy Frenchman, how long will you keep that smirk when the torture begins? Let's get to the point. I want Edouard Bonhomme—the man you call 'Rémi.' Tell me where he is and you go free."

Théo bit his lower lip.

"Once again. Tell me what I want, and you walk free. No cuts, no broken bones, no burns. If you defy me, well ... I'll just have to persuade you. Pay attention, I can be very inventive."

Théo closed his eyes and took a deep breath.

"Remove his shirt," the commander ordered. "We wouldn't want to soil it."

A guard slipped behind Théo, grabbed his shirt, and ripped it from his back. A quick snap filled the air as a whip wrapped around Théo's neck, biting into his skin. Warm blood trickled down his chest. He imagined a bright red necklace where the lash had cut into his throat. Stumbling forward, he caught himself before falling.

Seconds passed. Again, the whip. This time across Théo's back. He clenched his fists and his eyes watered. Another lash caused his teeth to lock, but he held his jaw steady. Saliva ran from the corners of his mouth.

"Oh, you are so brave, *Monsieur* Théo. But it is pointless. None of your friends will come for you. You can scream, but they won't hear. So, answer me, where can I find Bonhomme? Then no more ... uh, persuasion. You'll be given food and allowed to sleep. *Comprenez-vous?*"

Théo squinted, his eyes narrow slits. "Your ancestors were Huns—murderous baboons. Nothing's changed."

The Hunter handed his kitten to a guard and sauntered towards Théo. He grinned, moved toward Théo and spat in his face.

The spittle ran down Théo's cheek. He didn't try to wipe it away. Just smiled. He wouldn't let The Hunter break him.

The interrogator nodded, and the guard lashed Théo's back again, slicing a foot-long gash in his flesh. A scream escaped from his throat, as he fell to his knees. Théo pressed his hands against the cold concrete, to steady himself. He imagined himself a dog that had offended its master.

"Oh, how proud we are." The Hunter turned to his minion and held up five fingers.

Five more lashes tore into Théo's back. Finally, he collapsed on the floor.

"The location of your leader, *monsieur*, and you go free. If not, you die a broken man, for nothing. What a shame."

Théo was silent.

"Take him back to his cage," The Hunter ordered. "Ask him the same question every hour throughout the night—where is Bonhomme? If he refuses, lash him again. He'll weaken. They always do."

The guards untied Théo's hands, gripped him under the arms, and dragged him to his cell. As they shoved him inside Théo heard the door lock. He fell to the floor. Bars enveloped him, like a caged bird. His cot was wedged into a corner. Just a frame and metal springs. Cold and barren. Bright overhead lights clicked on, burning his eyes. More torture.

A gut-wrenching scream broke the silence. The Englishman was pulled to the center of the room, and dropped at The Hunter's feet.

Théo pressed his hands to his ears, horrified, knowing what was coming. How much more could the pilot take?

The Hunter kicked at the Brit's head. "You there! Why did you fly over France? Reconnaissance for an invasion, perhaps?"

"I d-don't know of any p-plans to invade. I'm just a pilot," the Brit sobbed. A long pause followed, then the sound of a whip. A scream, then cries. "I, I fly in and out of France." He gasped. "Supposed to do it in one night. Got lost. C-crashed," he whimpered.

"Well then, my skinny friend, do you often fly just for the fun of it—over *German territory*?" The Hunter said, snickering. The Englishman wept.

"I suspect you know more than you're telling," The Hunter said, turning his hand over and inspecting his nails.

"Let's see if this helps your memory." He signaled one of the guards to kick Giles.

The sickening sound of cracking ribs filled the air.

Three kicks, but no cries. The Englishman had fainted, face down on the concrete.

Guards dragged him back to his cell, dropped him on the floor, and locked the door.

The sound of heavy boots paraded through the basement. Théo heard them mount a flight of stairs, open and close a door, then silence. The Gestapo were gone but the brittle white light filled the cages.

***

"We have something special for you today," The Hunter said, as a guard pulled Théo from his cell. The interrogator was in the center of the room—where he stood yesterday—near the chair, the bright light overhead. The kitten, no longer in his arms.

"Let's start again," he said. "Your truck says '*plombier*' on the side. Seems to be freshly painted. Shall I assume this is your trade?"

"*Je suis un plombier*," Théo said. "It is my profession."

"Ah, then you are used to putting your head into stinking holes?" The Hunter said.

A large bucket of water was placed in front of Théo.

"Oh, but the water is clean. What a shame. We'll have to dirty it for you."

The guards unbuttoned their pants, stood over the pail, and peed. "I've been holding that for you," one guard said, laughing.

A second guard kicked Théo from behind. He fell

forward onto the concrete floor, missing the pail. Someone grabbed him by the hair and plunged his head into the bucket—holding him there. Théo tried to pull up, but failed. Foul water filled his mouth. The guard finally jerked him up. He gagged and choked.

Théo blinked the filthy water from his eyes. The guards stood over him, laughing.

"Now, are you ready to tell me what I want to know, or shall we repeat the game?" The Hunter asked.

"I don't know where Rémi is," Théo said, coughing. "Why don't you look for him in Paris?"

"Ha! Don't play with me."

Théo felt the crushing blow of a boot to his side. He grabbed at his ribs. Broken? He didn't know.

"Push his head in the bucket again. Longer this time," The Hunter said.

Théo struggled to wrench free, but couldn't. They were drowning him. Darkness closed in just as they pulled him up.

He choked and vomited. A boot came down on his back. His face pressed against the vomit-splattered concrete.

"Empty the bucket on the back of his head," The Hunter said.

Théo gagged and tried to pull away. The welts stung as the putrid water flowed into the raw gashes.

"Throw him in his cell and bring in the hoses. He needs a bath," The Hunter said, laughing.

Chapter 25
Intelligence
Vence

Rémi and the *maquisards* stood around a weathered table in the old farmhouse.

While waiting for Rémi to return, they'd begun making plans to rescue Théo and the Brit. Patrick had secured floor plans of the Gestapo headquarters. He spread them out on the table, for everyone to see.

"Who gave you these drawings?" Rémi asked, flipping through the diagrams on the table. He hated to be suspicious, but after being betrayed in Grasse he had no choice.

"Philippe, a *maquisard*. He works as a custodian in the Gestapo headquarters in Nice. He lives in the hotel—a requirement," Patrick said. "But he's getting anxious. They let him out once a week, but guards follow him. He has to be very careful exchanging information. When we go in for Théo, we'll need to bring Philippe out too," Patrick said.

"Where did he get the plans," Rémi asked.

"He drew them—knows the old building by heart," Patrick added.

"Understand this—after Grasse, I can't trust anyone I don't know," Rémi said.

"Philippe was my father's best friend," Patrick said, his voice cracking. "I've known him all my life. My father died in his arms after they failed to blow up the bridge over the Var. I'd trust him with my life."

"You're trusting him with all of our lives," Rémi said. "Have you considered that?"

"Yes," Patrick said.

The room went deathly silent. They all stared at Rémi. He had no choice but to trust the family friend.

Rémi nodded, moving back to the drawings—he studied them.

"I remember this building," Rémi said. "It's the old Hermitage Hotel. My family dined there on special occasions. I remember the double-door entrance. It's across from the Promenade, opposite the beach."

Rémi riffled through the sketches, reviewing them in rapid succession—from the ground floor to the fifth. "These are authentic—at least the ground floor, where the restaurant is located. Where are Théo and the Brit?"

"Right here," Patrick said pulling out one more diagram. "In the basement. It's where they cage all the prisoners."

Rémi listened and watched.

"The back entrance opens onto the parking lot. Deliveries are routinely made and rubbish removed.

Philippe says it's in constant use, and not heavily guarded."

"Not well guarded? Why not?" Charlotte asked.

"The *Boches*, especially the Gestapo, don't think anyone would *want* to get inside. After all, no prisoner has left alive—a rescue never tried," Patrick said.

"Then we have an advantage, don't we?" Charlotte said, smiling. "Intelligence defeats arrogance." Her eyes lit up—filled with hope.

Jules nodded. "I agree. We can overcome the bastards, with the right plan."

"Tell us how each floor is used," Rémi asked. "The Gestapo is known to segregate their activities."

"Each floor is guarded by two soldiers. The basement is the exception, where six Germans are on duty at all times. The old lobby, on the ground floor, is where prisoners are brought. Meetings are held in adjoining rooms. The first and second floors are Gestapo offices and sleeping quarters," Patrick explained.

"And the upper floors?" Rémi asked.

"Female prisoners are held on the third. It's currently empty. The fourth is usually packed with Jews, waiting to be deported. It's also empty. The fifth floor houses the maids and custodian."

"Let's take a closer look at the basement layout," Robin said.

"It's both a prison and torture chamber," Patrick pointed at the drawing. "The room is a rectangle, with concrete walls, floor, and ceiling. It's lined with cages—cells—where the prisoners are kept. Philippe confirmed that Théo and the Englishman are against the south wall, next to each other. As of yesterday, they were both alive."

Charlotte bit her lip, her eyes tearing.

"Where are the keys?" Marie asked.

"Philippe says the keys hang from a metal pole in the center of the room," Patrick added.

"Is it possible to rescue Théo *and* destroy the Gestapo headquarters?" Robin asked. The men stared at him. This was a new idea.

"I'm suggesting we blow the damned building up as soon as we rescue Théo and the others," Robin continued. "I want to kill the Gestapo butchers and all of their henchmen—every one of them."

Rémi nodded slowly, rubbing his chin—mulling the idea. "We'll need more men. Consider this: we stop a delivery truck before it reaches the headquarters. Tie up the drivers. Toss them in the back. Take their uniforms and drive into the parking lot. Overpower the guards when they come to the door. Four of us enter the basement from the back door."

"The initial attack must be completely silent," Patrick said. "Otherwise we alert the Gestapo on upper floors. They'll attack before we've freed the men."

"Agreed," Rémi said. "No shooting, if we can help it. Knives first. Guns later."

"Philippe told me that every other day, around midnight, a garbage truck stops in the parking lot and picks up trash bins. We'll intercept it," Patrick added, "and impersonate the drivers."

"So where are we in that schedule," Jules asked.

"I'll check with Philippe, but I seem to remember they pick up tomorrow, at midnight," Patrick said.

Pointing at the drawing, Patrick explained, "Philippe confirmed what Rémi said, the front doors are on the south side of the hotel. They open into a large circular lobby. Two Germans guard outside, one inside. Once we've secured the basement, we'll fire two shots from the parking lot, alerting our second team to kill the guards, enter the front doors, and take control of the lobby."

"*Bon,*" Rémi said. "This has to be timed perfectly or we won't stand a chance."

"Once inside the basement," Patrick added, "we'll try to lock the door leading up to the lobby. If we can't do that, we'll position two of our men where they can shoot anyone trying to escape from the floors above. We create a lockdown, with the Gestapo upstairs unable to get out."

"Perfect. Philippe must be on the ground floor when we enter, along with any maids from the fifth. That's the only way we can save them," Rémi warned. "Altogether, it looks like we need at least six more men. I'll work on that. I know some trusted *maquisards,* in Nice. I'll contact them today."

"I'll package the explosives," Jules said. "We'll require two men laying the plastique on the east and west sides of the hotel while the rescue is going on."

"Two escape vehicles are needed, initially parked

around the corner and out of sight. Once the drivers hear gunshots they can reposition the vans next to headquarters," Rémi said. "Those of us extracting Théo and the Brit will transfer the men to one of the vans and pile in with them. When the long fuses are lit, the *maquisards* will have to run for the second van, along with Philippe and the maids. Both vans immediately head to the Nice marina.

"Charlotte, work with Marie on securing the two trucks. Robin, arrange for a good-sized boat to pick us up," Rémi ordered. "And find a coastal village where we can hide for a month or so. Given the past week, it seems the Falicon *Maquis* are the Gestapo's prime target. We need to disappear."

Rémi felt his confidence return. The plan was solid—save Théo and destroy the Gestopo. His team could do it.

Charlotte drew a deep breath, and let it out slowly. "I'm afraid Théo has little time."

"We'll check with Philippe, but it looks like we'll attack tomorrow night," Rémi said.

He glanced around the room, locking eyes with the *maquisards*.

"We *won't* fail."

Chapter 26
Arrogance
Gestapo Headquarters, Nice

Fire hoses blasted Théo from one side of his cell to the other. Guards aimed the water at his lacerated back—ripping the wounds open. He curled into a ball on the floor and cupped his hands around his nose and mouth, trying to breathe. For the second time in as many days, he was certain they'd drown him.

As suddenly as the water turned on, it turned off. The Gestapo moved to the Englishman's cell. The Brit was delirious—had been tossing and mumbling for the past four hours. Théo watched as the guards turned both nozzles on high. Giles didn't utter a word. He didn't even hold up his hands to protect his face. A merciful death—if he drowned.

The guards did the same to all the prisoners. Only when the water pressure gave out did they stop.

Théo thought he heard the guards leave. "Can you hear me? Are you alive?" Théo asked the Brit. No answer, just moaning. "Don't give up."

A voice bellowed from a dark corner of the basement. "If you can talk to the Englishman, you can talk to us," The Hunter said.

Théo thought they'd left. Did his hearing fail? Maybe this is what happens when the body shuts down.

"Isn't there an expression in the Bible—something about 'the fire next time'? You've survived water. I think it's time for fire. Pull him out," The Hunter ordered. "Throw him over there, next to the brazier. On the floor, face down, pants off."

The guards stripped Théo and dragged him across the room.

"Now, Théo-Hugo, whatever your name is—I'll ask again, *where* is your leader?" Silence. "Let me put it another way. Where would *you* go if you were free? Falicon? I don't think so. We burned your house down. Nothing left. What about Tourrettes? No."

The Hunter wagged his finger, mockingly. "They are too frightened to hide an important *maquisard*. Perhaps Vence? Very close, very convenient, wouldn't you say? But my men have searched. Your leader isn't there.

"Pull his head back," The Hunter ordered a guard. "I want him to see the iron before he smells his flesh burn."

The Hunter waved a branding iron in front of Théo's face. "A swastika. You'll wear it, just as I wear this little pin on my lapel. It's rather attractive, don't you think?"

Théo felt the heat. The branding iron was only inches from his face.

The Hunter gestured toward a guard. "You. Hold the *Frog* down." Handing the branding iron to a second guard, The Hunter stepped away. Just as Théo recalled—he was a sadistic observer.

"Now," he ordered, "press it, hard, onto his buttocks."

Théo felt his flesh burn. His hands clenched, fingernails cutting into his palms. The pain.... He gulped for air, but refused to cry out.

"The other side. We want him to feel it, every time he sits, walks, moves." The Hunter ordered.

Théo's chest tightened as excruciating pain shot through him. His heart would stop. He was certain. No man could stand this torture. He screamed, high-pitched and long. It filled the basement. He choked and gagged, holding back a sob before it escaped his lips.

"Throw him back in his cage. Bring me the Englishman. Let's send him off to hell if he hasn't already gone."

From inside his cell, Théo rolled into a ball. The pain excruciating—the bitter cold chilled him until he shook. He smelled burnt flesh—his own.

Théo didn't think the Englishman would survive. He forced himself to crawl to the bars, and watch. The Brit didn't cry out. Didn't even flinch. Perhaps the branding killed him, or he was dead already.

"Throw the carcass in with the Frenchman. When he begins to rot, the smell will drive *monsieur* Théo to confess," The Hunter said, laughing.

Two more prisoners were branded before the night was over. Ceaseless screaming and sobbing filled the air.

***

Théo lay face down on his cot. He shivered violently. The chattering of his teeth kept him from hearing someone approach.

Philippe whispered, "Théo. I have a message from the *Maquis*."

Théo lifted his head. His vision blurred—his hearing muffled. A figure in drab gray, the kind worn by custodial staff, stood outside his cell.

"Come," Philippe coaxed. "I'm a *maquisard*. I have a note from Rémi."

Théo struggled to his feet. "Rémi?" He lost his balance and fell to his knees.

"*Oui,*" Philippe said, waiting for Théo to accept the message.

Théo took the note and crawled back to the cot. Unfolding the message, he stood and squinted at the text. Trying to focus. "We come at midnight." Signed by Rémi. The message was real.

Théo tore the paper into tiny pieces, chewed and swallowed them, nearly heaving the dry fragments.

He woke a few hours later, still shaking violently. Was it day or night? He couldn't tell. The Hunter's heavy boots tramped across the concrete. It must be daytime. The Hunter never came at night. But was it morning or afternoon? Had he imagined the man in gray? He tasted paper in his mouth.

The Hunter stood at the entrance to Théo's cell. "Oh, my poor naked bird. We don't want you to die before you tell us about Bonhomme. Take this blanket. One of the prisoners left it for you," he said, snickering. "Say a little prayer for him. He's probably in your Purgatory by now."

The Hunter signaled his guards to pull Théo back to the brazier. They thrust him into the bloodstained chair in the center of the room. Théo screamed. The blistered brands oozed.

"Make yourself comfortable. Tell me about our girlfriend. Her parents live on a small farm just outside Torino. Oh pardon me, they *lived* on a farm. They betrayed their country. They're in prison now."

Why did he have to bring Charlotte into this? Théo's head went limp.

The Hunter snapped his fingers in front of Théo's nose and yelled, "Listen carefully. All I need to do is contact the Torino Gestapo, and the traitors will be shot."

He leaned in. His lips only inches from Théo's face. "The parents will live if your girlfriend turns herself in. She'll never forgive you if she knows you let her mother and father die. So, where oh where has the daughter gone?" he asked, mockingly.

"D-d-don't know." Théo's voice croaked with fatigue and pain. "You burned the farmhouse. Don't know where she is."

"Well, well, well. Since you have nothing to add, I

will just have to line you up with the others in the morning, and bang, bang, bang. All dead. No more torture." With a flip of his hand, he stomped out of the room. The guards dragged Théo back into his cell, dumped him on the metal cot, and covered him with the blanket.

Within hours, Théo was scratching furiously. He looked down at his arms. They were covered with tiny black specks. Fleas! The blanket was full of them. He scrambled up, lost his balance, and fell to the floor. Grabbing the blanket, he covered the dead Englishman, hoping to muffle the smell.

Théo crawled to the far corner of the cage. He had to get away from the body. Naked and shivering, he tried to brush the fleas off. His fever grew worse. Perhaps he would die soon. Cheat the Gestapo out of killing him in the morning.

Rescue—a false hope.

Chapter 27
Midnight
Gestapo Headquarters, Nice

Rémi fled from Grasse so he could rescue Théo. He *had* to succeed.

A thin slice of the moon hovered above the sea as the band of *maquisards* moved silently through the dark streets of Nice. Four would enter the basement from the parking lot, kill the guards, and take Théo. The others would neutralize the Gestapo inside headquarters and set the explosives.

Two blocks from the headquarters, Rémi positioned himself in the center of an adjacent street. A large garbage collection truck lumbered toward him.

"Arrêtez!" Rémi yelled, pointing his rifle at the driver. He held his position as a screech of brakes and a rough grinding of gears brought the truck to a stop. Patrick leapt from the shadows and jerked the driver's door open. Rémi did the same on the passenger side.

"Get out," Rémi ordered. "Open the back doors and

get inside."

Gagged, the drivers were stripped of their clothes, and tied up. Rémi and Patrick pulled on the uniforms and climbed into the front seat. Marie and Charlotte trotted behind the vehicle, using it as cover.

Rémi muscled the truck into the headquarters parking lot, stopping at the receiving door and basement entrance. Wiping his sweating palms on his pants, he took a deep breath. Two armed guards stood beside the raised door—trash bins ready to be loaded.

Patrick and Rémi climbed out of the truck and approached the guards. The *maquisards* offered their papers. The guards cradled their rifles in the crook of their left arms and reached for the identification.

Two daggers flashed in the moonlight. The guards fell to the ground—throats slashed. "Pull them out of the way," Rémi said. "Other guards will come."

Hidden in the shadows, the two men waited.

"Why are you taking so long?" a German bellowed from inside.

"The trash is heavy," Patrick yelled in German. Sliding behind a bin, he began pushing it.

"Awk! You French have no muscle," yelled the guard, dropping his gun and bending over to push the container. "But where are the other guards?" he asked. "Why aren't they helping?"

Patrick thrust his knife deep into the soldier's back. The *Boche* gasped. A soft cry passed through his lips before he fell to the ground.

"What's going on?" another guard yelled. "There

wasn't that much trash!"

Rémi caught sight of him, near the overhead light in the basement. Charlotte's blade whizzed past Rémi's ear.

"*Merde*," he heard her whisper. "Only grazed him."

Rifle in hand, the guard shot back. Charlotte tossed Rémi his gun. He fired. They heard a scream, then silence.

Another guard shot from the right, behind a cage—a prisoner on the floor. Marie crouched, and fired through the bars. The guard collapsed.

"There's one more," Rémi yelled. "Philippe said there'd be six guards. Over there!" Rémi pointed. "The last one. He's heading toward the stairs leading to the lobby! Stop him!"

Patrick took aim, and shot. "He's down!"

Marie remained at the back door, guarding the *maquisards*. No need to signal the men upstairs to enter the lobby. Shots had already been fired.

Patrick ran into the basement. Making his way to the other side of the room, he found the door to the lobby and shoved the bolt in place.

Charlotte and Rémi searched for Théo—checking the cells on the south wall.

"Here he is," she yelled. "Get the keys."

Théo shivered in the corner of the cell. Naked. He looked disoriented—in shock.

Rémi pulled the keys from the hook and tossed them to her. "I brought some pants. Gestapo strip prisoners."

A fierce gun battle sounded overhead. It was taking longer than anticipated to neutralize the Gestapo. The loading dock gunfire alerted them.

"Unlock the door. *Vite!*" Rémi yelled at Charlotte.

"Too many keys. Haven't found ... here it is!"

Rémi looked for Patrick. "Over here! We need your help," Rémi yelled, nodding toward the cells. "Find the Brit."

Charlotte's hands shook as she opened the door.

"Oh my God—the Brit," she said, gagging.

"*Putain,*" Rémi said. "Gestapo. Bastards!"

"Help us, Patrick. The Brit's dead," Rémi said.

"Charlotte?" Théo's voice croaked.

"I'm here," she said, stepping into the cell. "Can you stand?" she asked, trying to help him up.

Rémi supported him, using the bars as a brace, while Charlotte helped Théo step into the pants. She heard him suck in air as the pants were pulled over the brands.

"No time for shoes or a shirt," Rémi said. "Get him into the van."

Charlotte and Rémi supported Théo. Patrick took hold of his legs and helped carry him to the van.

The lobby had quieted. Rémi glanced back at the hotel. Just as planned, *maquisards* were placing plastique and fuses around the building. Adrenaline churned through Rémi's body—sending a chill down his arms. God willing, they'd pull this off.

They lifted Théo into the van, then followed him in. Rémi wrapped him in a blanket. Charlotte cradled

Théo in her lap.

"The second van just pulled up behind us," Marie said. "The men are loading."

Sirens wailed nearby. "Go!" Rémi yelled at the driver.

The van fishtailed onto the Promenade, with the second one following right behind.

Two Germans on motorcycles sped out of a side street. They fired low, trying to hit the vehicle's tires.

Rémi and the others were jostled side to side as their driver zigzagged his way along the Promenade and around the promontory toward the marina.

A large motorboat waited, along with four armed *maquisards*. Two quick shots took out the cyclists—one slammed into a warehouse, the second arched into the bay.

The vans screeched to a halt. Two men with rifles stood guard, while the other two helped load the boat.

"*Sirènes! Allez-y!*" a man hissed.

As Rémi stepped into the boat, a massive explosion consumed the night. The wave of pressure nearly knocked him to the floor. A billowing fireball rose above the promontory, illuminating the sky from Antibes to Eze. The Gestapo and their headquarters—gone in a fiery blaze.

A cheer filled the air.

"Let's go," Rémi yelled.

They spun out of the marina. Lights off, at a speed just shy of flipping the boat. A low canvas roof protected Rémi and his team. Charlotte crouched low beside Théo, bracing him against the boat's motion.

As they rounded the promontory, they looked to their right. An inferno consumed Gestapo headquarters.

"We did it!" Rémi said. The *maquisards* cheered once more.

With heads low, they gripped the sides of the boat, bobbing over dark waters and out into the bay.

Rémi pulled Marie against his chest. Drawing her head under his chin, he protected her from spraying water. So much could have gone wrong, but it didn't. The Gestapo were dead, their fortress destroyed.

Nearly an hour passed before the pilot spoke. "We're approaching Port du Niel, near Iles d'Hyères. It's a good hiding place for boats and people. Less than a kilometer from the Hôspital San Salvadour. If your man needs help, I know a doctor."

"*Merci.*" Rémi nodded.

They pulled into the marina. Two men waited, ready to tie the boat and escort them to a new hideout.

Patrick helped Charlotte with Théo. Rémi and Marie scrambled after them.

Just off the marina, they entered a narrow alley between two stone buildings. Rémi took Charlotte's place, helping Patrick with Théo. Each man stretched an arm around Théo, his feet barely touching the ground. He groaned but didn't speak, as they dragged him along the path.

Within a hundred meters, they exited to a small path that cut through an apple orchard. Five minutes later they arrived at a sheltered house—one story and low to the ground—nearly indistinguishable from the surroundings.

The escorts showed Rémi a bedroom where Théo could recover. Everyone except Rémi, Marie, and Charlotte collapsed in the living room.

Rémi helped the women wash Théo with warm herbal water, dabbing at his wounds. Finally, they applied Marie's salve to his back, and then turned to the terrible burns.

Rémi glanced at Marie—worried.

"He hasn't said a word. I want him to take some broth or tea before he sleeps. Will you see if our hosts have some?" Marie asked.

"Certainly. But those brands...."

"We'll find a doctor tomorrow," Charlotte said, shuddering. "He must not die, not now, not after this."

"He will live," Rémi said, "but he'll be a different man."

Chapter 28
Anticipating Spring
Port du Niel, France

Charlotte never left Théo's side. She slept in a chair next to his bed, waiting for him to talk. A week passed and Théo hadn't said a word. Rémi told her to talk to him, even if he didn't answer.

She leaned over Théo's bed and kissed him on the cheek. "I love you," she whispered. "I need you. France needs you. If you don't continue to fight, the Gestapo has won. They've destroyed your dreams of a free France and taken your soul."

Each day she ministered to his wounds, fed him, and changed his bedclothes. He was slowly healing—physically. The wounds on his back had developed minor infections, but they were treated and cured within days. New skin formed.

The brands took longer to heal. The doctor from the nearby hospital suggested skin grafts. But that could wait. "No reason to bring more pain and agony to this young man. Not now, anyway."

One night, deep in the darkness that winter holds, Charlotte sat beside Théo singing from a hymnal—the only book she could find in the farmhouse. She kept her voice soft and low, so as not to wake the others. Stopping for a moment, she replaced a sputtering candle, set the book in her lap, and closed her eyes.

She was drifting off to sleep when she felt a hand on hers and a softly whispered, "Charlotte."

"Théo!" She took his hand and held it to her lips. "Théo, you've returned."

He nodded. "From a world of nightmares." He lay on his stomach, his face turned toward her. Charlotte sank to her knees beside him. "We will chase the nightmares away—you and I."

A weak smile crossed his lips and he sighed deeply. "Yes, we will." He squeezed her hand.

"May I wake the men and bring them in?"

"*Oui*," he said. "Bring them in. They saved my life and I want to thank them."

***

A week later, after the others had gone to bed, Charlotte talked to Théo about the brands. "If you'd like, the doctor can remove them with skin grafts. They will take some time to heal, and infection can be a problem. You might be in the hospital for quite a while."

"I'll keep them until the war is over," Théo said. "They fuel my hatred of the *Boches*. I feel the brands every time I sit and walk. I want to remember how the

Gestapo tortured me and killed the Englishman. When France is free, I'll have the brands removed. Then I'll allow the memories to fade, if I can."

Charlotte nodded, remembering what Rémi said. *He'll live, but he'll be a different man.* Could Théo ever let go of his bitter memories, or would they haunt him for a lifetime?

***

Throughout the winter months, Charlotte worked with Théo to regain his strength. He even laughed from time to time. They joined the men for meals and took short walks. The cold bit the skin, and the days were short, but she insisted on getting outside and breathing fresh air. "It is good for you," she repeated. "And it gives color to your cheeks. You're getting stronger—every day."

They often slipped into a small copse of trees near the edge of the orchard, held each other and kissed, enjoying the warmth of the other's touch. One afternoon while a quiet snow fell, Théo pulled Charlotte into the trees and let his hands roam under her coat and across her body, lightly touching her breasts.

"I love you," he said, pressing himself against her. "I want to make love to you now, here among the trees."

"Can we do it standing up?" she asked, innocently. "It would be awfully cold on the ground."

"But of course we can stand." He smiled. "Just lean against the tree. Be as quiet as you can. We mustn't wake the squirrels."

Their hunger for each other came to a rapid climax.

Charlotte's eyes remained closed as he put her skirt back in order.

"Umm. Let me dress you now," she said, opening her eyes. "I did it many times when you were sleeping. I washed you too."

"You are a tease, *mon amour,*" he said, laughing. "I'll let you help me next time."

Charlotte smoothed out her coat and tidied herself. "I think it's time for some hot tea," she said.

They walked arm-in-arm back to the farmhouse. Théo pushed the door open and entered. Everyone was there. No one spoke.

Théo and Charlotte glanced at each other. A question on their faces. They shook the snow from their coats and hung them by the door, then turned toward the *maquisards.*

Something *was* different. The house, often filled with men planning and rehearsing new missions, was hauntingly quiet.

"What is it?" Charlotte asked. "Why are you all so somber?"

"Charlotte, I need to speak with you. Let's talk in the kitchen," Rémi said.

Charlotte felt her stomach roil. Something terrible had happened. She released her hand from Théo's, and stumbled into the kitchen.

"Please, sit," Rémi said, closing the kitchen door.

She bit her lip.

When they were both seated, he placed a letter on the table. "I received this from my father today. He enclosed a message from the Menton *Maquis*."

He reached for her hand, held it tightly, and looked her in the eye. "Your parents, Charlotte. They were shot and killed two weeks ago."

"No," she whispered. "No, no," she said, shaking her head. "I don't believe it! Not *my* mother and father."

"It's true. I wish it weren't, but it is," Rémi said.

She bent over the table, sobbing gut-wrenching cries that wouldn't stop.

Marie and Théo entered the kitchen, and hugged her, but even they couldn't help.

"It's my fault. They're dead because of me," she wailed.

"No, Charlotte," Rémi said, "It's not because of you or anything the *Maquis* may have done. Your parents were not singled out. The Nazis killed everyone in the village, declaring them a nest of traitors—anti-fascists. They burned all their homes and destroyed their fields."

Charlotte lifted her head, face streaked with tears and eyes red from crying. "*Mon Dieu*," she sobbed, shaking her head.

Time passed, and she quieted. Swallowing hard, she turned to Théo. "I *must* go back to Torino."

"No," Rémi said, grasping her hand. "That's what the Germans want. They'll watch for you, knowing you'd want to visit your home—say a prayer over your parents' grave. It would be suicide."

"Now I understand why my father insisted I leave Italy. This is what he feared most," Charlotte said.

Théo pulled her into his arms, holding her. She clutched him tightly.

Marie and Rémi wrapped their arms around the couple.

"You are my family," Charlotte said, choking. "You're all I have."

Chapter 29
**White Fox and the *Maquis*
Port du Niel**

That evening over hot soup and warm bread, Rémi shared the good news. He was glad to break the pall cast by the fate of Charlotte's parents. "I've heard from the Cannes *Maquis*," he said. "An Allied invasion is imminent, somewhere on the north coast—maybe Calais."

The *Maquis* cheered loudly. "At last," Jules said, rubbing his hands together.

Rémi held up his palm. "We won't know until a day or two beforehand. Don't speak openly of it in the cafés. We've got to keep it secret from the Germans.

"But while we wait, I have information that could change our lives forever. A second offensive in the center of France is planned at Clermont-Ferrand. There is also talk of an offensive in Vercors—closer to the German border."

"What about the Riviera?" Patrick asked. "That's

still a possibility, isn't it?"

"Yes. I'm certain of that, but not before the west coast invasion," Rémi answered. "For now, let me share what I know about counteroffensive from within France. There is a call for *maquisards* to gather in Clermont-Ferrand. Thousands of *Maquis* have already committed."

"Who will lead them? Coordination will be hard, we're so spread out and independent," Robin said.

Rémi lit a cigarette and leaned back. "I've heard the White Fox will return from England. Wireless says she'll arrive in Clermont-Ferrard within the month. With her leadership, the *Maquis* will win. The British want us to destabilize the German war machine. Hit them on the west coast, the center, and the south of France—within a month or two of each other. The British and Americans have promised help—guns and munitions. Air support, too, and soldiers."

"Tell me about the White Fox," Charlotte said. "Why do the *Maquis* follow her?"

"She's legendary," Marie offered. "The Resistance reveres her. She was born in Australia, immigrated to London, then came to Paris to work for a newspaper. I've seen pictures. She's beautiful—short curly black hair, very slim. She fell in love with our country, speaks French perfectly, married an industrialist, and settled in Marseille."

"She doesn't sound like the type to lead a band of *maquisards* against the *Boches*," Charlotte said.

"She changed very suddenly," Rémi said, taking a

drag on his cigarette. "She went to Germany in 1938, as a freelance journalist. Some Parisians wondered what was happening there, and wanted answers. She saw Nazi brutality firsthand. When she returned, she wrote about the Brownshirts who rampaged through the streets humiliating Jews, gypsies, and other foreigners. People were beaten, and shops raided. Worst of all she witnessed the cult of Hitler. Swastikas ... everywhere, and '*Sieg Heil*' on everyone's lips. She decided to do whatever she could to defend her adopted country."

"But she is just one woman. What could she do?" Charlotte asked.

"That woman is like an army of men," Théo laughed.

Rémi nodded. "Her love of France and the fear of increasing German violence motivated her. She wrote articles, but they weren't enough. People didn't take the German threat seriously. Then it was too late."

"She was very courageous," Marie said. "Traveling to Germany by herself—she could have been captured or killed."

"You're right," Rémi said. "After the Germans occupied France, kidnapping became frequent. Friends of the White Fox began disappearing—taken by Nazis to secret places, questioned and tortured. People lived in constant fear. When her husband disappeared, she immediately joined the Resistance."

"Did her husband survive?" Charlotte asked.

"He was tortured and died," Rémi said. "When the White Fox learned of his death, she was determined to kill the man responsible. She took a great chance and invited the head of the Gestapo, Klaus von Blick, to her home in Marseille. Surprisingly, he came—without guards."

Charlotte leaned in, her eyes sparkled with interest.

"She served him expensive wine and French delicacies. Just as he was growing groggy from food and drink, she approached him from behind and strangled him with a cord," Marie said.

"*Mon Dieu.* Seems impossible," Charlotte said.

"It's the stuff of legends," Rémi said, smiling. "But this we know for certain, from that night on she worked full time with the Resistance, and never returned to her home. She was fierce—never shying away, not even from the most dangerous assignments. The Gestapo listed her as their most wanted enemy, and posted a five million franc reward."

"She outsmarted them like a fox," Charlotte said.

"Yes, but she *was* captured several times—but always escaped. I heard she broke out of one prison by stripping naked and slithering through the bars." Rémi exhaled a puff of smoke and turned his hand front to back. "Perhaps this is another legend—who knows? But, she *did* escape."

"She must have been very thin!" Jules laughed.

"Ah, but there is more to this story," Rémi said. "She carries a dagger, like yours Charlotte. A pistol, too, but she prefers the knife. Many say she's one of the fiercest fighters they've ever seen. There are *Maquis* who won't go into battle without her."

"She's a modern *Jeanne d'Arc*," Patrick said.

"*Maquisards* who've worked with her say she is fierce under fire, and always makes the tough decisions. She once killed a female double agent when none of the men would do it. Dragged her into a field and shot her in the head." Rémi shuddered. "She has no equal."

"I remember," Charlotte said, "when I first arrived, you wanted me to meet with her."

"About that time," Rémi said, "Marseille became too dangerous for us to enter. Collaborators were everywhere. Some would sell their soul for the reward. About six months ago, she escaped over the Pyrenees into Spain—finally making her way to London. We pieced all this together from Special Operations Executives who were flown in from France, and also from wireless messages.

"Prime Minister Churchill asked her to remain in London, where she could be trained in espionage. Some say the SOE is Churchill's private army, and the White Fox his personal spy," Rémi added.

"She seems too perfect. Any flaws?" Charlotte asked.

"Well, I don't consider it a flaw," Rémi said, winking at Marie. "I've heard she travels in a small bus with a built-in bed and sleeps in a negligée between silk sheets. She retains her femininity despite her ruthlessness."

"Will we fight with the White Fox?" Charlotte asked, eagerly.

"This spring may be too soon for the Riviera

Maquis to mobilize. But I hear there could be a second offensive in Vercors. The White Fox will let us know, once she arrives. The delay will give us time to gather guns, ammunition, and recruit more *maquisards*. Keep in mind, Vercors is about two hundred kilometers from Nice, and we no longer have a truck. We'll have to walk."

Rémi turned to his *maquisards*, "I'll need every one of you to fight like five men, just like the White Fox."

***

The White Fox parachuted into northern Auvergne in April. She immediately began building an army. Just as forecast, her command center was Clermont-Ferrand, south of Vichy, near the Monts Domes.

The *Maquis* quickly learned her mission: divert Germany's attention from the west coast. Make the Germans think *this* is the primary invasion—the beginning point of the Allies' major offensive against Germany.

As the *Maquis* kept abreast of the activities in Clermont-Ferrand, Riviera *maquisards* continued to sabotage German transport trains—taking weapons and ammunition. The Falicon *Maquis* commandeered trucks—shipping guns north to Vercors in anticipation of a second offensive. The White Fox mobilized over 8,000 *maquisards* for the attack against the German army near Clermont-Ferrand. The British were quick to supply the White Fox with guns and artillery. Food and medical supplies were also flown in.

Then came the day they'd been waiting for. On the second of June, 1944 the White Fox and her men attacked 20,000 German soldiers. It was a long hard battle, but at the end of the day the French won, overwhelmingly. The Germans lost fourteen hundred men. The *maquisards* lost four-hundred—a triumph for the Allies.

The *Boches* were outmaneuvered. But most of all they'd been forced to take their eye off the Channel coast. Four days later, on June 6, the Allies struck Normandy. The battle for Europe had begun.

***

Soon after her victory, The White Fox messaged the Riviera *Maquis* to prepare to fight the Germans in Vercors, suggesting an early July offensive. She assured them that Churchill and the Americans would support them with guns and supplies. Message sent, she returned to London.

But it was also whispered, among the Maquis, that a second attack on the Germans within such a short time would demonstrate the revival of the French military and cause the *Boches* to retreat back to their original borders.

Riviera *Maquis* began departing for Vercors. But everyone was curious. Who would lead them in this counteroffensive, and if their goal was the same as that of the White Fox, why hadn't she stayed?

In early July, Rémi and the Falicon *Maquis* began their trek to Vercors. They were often picked up by *maquisards* and transported five or ten kilometers along their route. It took them a week to reach Vercors but they were able to gather information along the way. They were completely taken by surprise when they heard the Vercors *Maquis* had declared independence from the occupying German army *and* from France.

"Why would they do such a thing?" Charlotte asked Rémi, as they sat at an evening campfire.

"Many believe France will fracture when the war is over. They see it dividing between de Gaulle's Free French army, the communists, Resistance fighters in the large cities, and the *Maquis*. De Gaulle fears this too, so he declared himself President of France. The communists and most Resistance workers don't like this," Théo said.

"So, the Vercors *Maquis* got ahead of everyone and declared independence from both France and Germany?" She asked.

"It's a dangerous move," Jules shook his head. "They've ignored the possibility of German retribution. It's like waving a red flag in front of a bull."

"It's done," Rémi added. "We can't change it."

As they walked toward Vercors, Charlotte felt the energy. Men were on the road all around them, not slinking through the woods and whispering. They were a noisy ragtag army. Excitement filled the air. Their chance to win a battle against the Germans was at hand. But more than that, it held the possibility of a German rout and the end of the Occupation.

But Charlotte worried, were they celebrating too soon?

Chapter 30
The Republic of Vercors
Village of Vassieux
July, 1944

Rémi was quick to embrace his friend Gaston, leader of the Vercors *Maquis*. A short grizzled man with a raspy voice. His hair floated about his head in a frazzled mess. His clothes were rumpled and he sported a two-week old beard, but Rémi knew that his mission was clear. Gaston loved his country above all else and would do anything to win it back.

"Glad you've arrived, *mon ami,*" Gaston said. "Men are pouring in from all corners of France, not just the Riviera. Some who fought with the White Fox have joined us too. Most *maquisards* brought guns and ammunition, but not all. Your shipments arrived, but we'll need a lot more. We expect airdrops from Britain soon, perhaps tonight. *Then* we'll be ready to fight the Germans—and win!

"Come, let's discuss strategy," Gaston said. "I've

called a meeting of the *Maquis* leaders. Your men can familiarize themselves with the area as we talk."

"I'll see you in a few hours," Rémi said, glancing over his shoulder at the Falicon *Maquis*.

***

"Let's explore the village and surrounding area," Charlotte said to Marie. "We need to know where the Germans might advance and how to escape, if necessary."

As they walked about Vassieux, and the meadowlands surrounding the small village, Charlotte began to worry.

"Is there only one road on the south side of the Vassieux?" Charlotte asked.

"Yes. It's the one we took to get here," Marie said. "But notice, there are valleys that lead away from Vercors. We could escape down the valleys, or take refuge in the caves. See them on the canyon walls?" Marie pointed to the landmarks.

"I see grottos where we could hide and pick off the *Boches*. Maybe we don't need to worry about blocked roads," Charlotte said.

The valley was surrounded by mountains—large and small. The women climbed to a saddle between two crests. "Where are the Germans?" Charlotte asked. "Rémi said they'd be camped in the surrounding valleys. But I don't hear or see them."

Charlotte pointed down the hill. "There is a small encampment, but nothing like the numbers we were told. Didn't Rémi say there'd be ten to twenty thousand

Germans?"

"They could be divided into different camps to throw us off guard—make it appear there are far less than expected," Marie said. "The *massif*, where we stand, is huge—perhaps 18,000 square meters. There are many mountains and more than one plateau. There is hardly a flat spot, except right here in the village of Vassieux," Marie said. "Until now, the Germans have left Vercors alone, but God only knows what they have in store for us. They've been humiliated by the White Fox, and by Vercors' declaration of independence."

"Gaston may be fooling himself. We could already be surrounded. That might explain why there weren't roadblocks coming in. Perhaps the Germans are just toying with us—drawing us in, then shutting the door behind."

"*Mon Dieu*," Marie exhaled. "What have we gotten ourselves into?"

***

It was dusk and the Falicon *Maquis* were camped in the woods, just beyond the village.

"We need the British guns and ammunition before Bastille Day. Without them...." Rémi wiped his forehead, "well, the British *must* help us."

"Charlotte and I saw only one road from the south. If that's blocked and the Germans attack by air. . . ." Marie's voice trailed off.

Rémi's eyes narrowed. "Don't speak of defeat. We must believe we'll win."

The *maquisards* grew silent. Marie looked away.

"Don't scold Marie," Charlotte challenged. "We need to prepare for all possibilities."

"Sorry," Rémi said. "I'm on edge. Watch the skies tonight and tomorrow. There's no reason to believe the British won't deliver."

Gaston entered the camp. "*Bonsoir*, my friends. We have two thousand *maquisards* gathered throughout Vercors. I'm distributing armbands." He handed Rémi bands marked with the Cross of Lorraine—a "V" at the tip of the cross. "It's our new flag. The Republic of Vercors. We haven't any uniforms, but these will do. Wear them up high on your arm, so they are easily seen. We don't want to shoot at our own people."

Eyeballing Marie and Charlotte, Gaston continued, "We'll set up a makeshift hospital in one of the large grottos. There are sure to be men who need medical attention. You'll work there."

"We will help the injured," Charlotte said, "but we'll also fight with the men."

Gaston looked at Rémi. "Is this true? They fight like the White Fox?"

Rémi nodded. "They're good with guns and knives. Don't worry. They've earned the right to wear the armband, as much as the rest of us."

Gaston lifted an eyebrow, then smiled. "Listen for the planes tonight. They'll drop the guns by parachute. Be ready to pull the cartons into the woods and camouflage them. Tomorrow we'll distribute."

Why are the British waiting so long? Rémi wondered. Tomorrow is Bastille Day.

Chapter 31
July 14, 1944
Bastille Day
Vercors, France

No guns or ammunition were delivered during the night, but nothing could stop the annual celebration of Bastille Day.

Charlotte smiled at Théo as he took her hand. "Good to be in Vassieux on this special day," she said. Théo nodded.

Maquisards and villagers gathered in the village center to celebrate the French revolution and the founding of a nation.

Gaston spoke from a small platform in the city square. "We will be rewarded," he said. "Don't forget what unifies us all: loyalty, courage, honor, and decency. This is *our* land and *our* nation. We *will* take it back!"

"*À votre santé!*" cried the *maquisards*, holding up small glasses of red wine. Someone began singing *La*

Marseillaise, and everyone joined in. Laughter and song echoed down the canyon walls, blanketing the valley floor.

But through the joy of celebration came a low and distant rumble. Charlotte looked to the sky. Billowing parachutes and cases of guns floated down from airplanes—along with paratroopers. "Look," she cried. "Weapons and soldiers!"

"At last!" Gaston yelled.

She squinted at the planes' insignia. "No! Wait. They're not British," she screamed. "They're German!"

"Grab your guns!" Gaston yelled. "Man the barricades. We'll pick them off as they charge the hill."

From behind hay bales, Charlotte watched as Germans touched down in a pasture just below the village. They discarded parachutes, pulled rifles from cases, and took cover behind stone outcroppings.

Another group of German soldiers set up a grenade launching machine. She watched, helpless, as a grenade catapulted over her head, hitting a building near the city square. A second lobbed near the church, taking out part of the road. The explosions turned walls to rubble and *maquisards* to rag dolls. Men were thrown into the air. Writhing in pain, their screams filled the village.

The German soldiers advanced toward them. "They're shooting at us from all sides," Charlotte cried. They'd been outmaneuvered and outnumbered in a matter of minutes.

"Take cover behind the buildings," Gaston yelled. "Keep your backs to the center of the village."

Mortars continued to blast the village, crushing walls and opening large holes in buildings. Timbers and rubble fell into the street, blocking vehicles. The villagers, celebratory only moments before, were now in a battle for their lives.

Charlotte fought alongside Théo, but their ammunition wouldn't last if the intense German barrage continued. "We can't defend the village. There are too many *Boches*," Charlotte yelled over the din. "And more are parachuting in."

"Retreat to the alley," Théo nodded to his right. "I have a few rounds left."

As they backed down a narrow alleyway, Théo reloaded his rifle. A German stepped into the alley and took aim. Charlotte threw her knife, hitting her mark— the German's stomach. He fell backward, screaming. A knife lodged in his belly.

Another soldier fired. Théo shot back, but his bullet went high. He fell to his knees, clutching his chest. Another bullet sliced the side of Théo's head. Blood covered him as he toppled to the ground.

The soldier took aim at Charlotte and pulled the trigger. The sound of a loud "click" filled the alleyway. Out of bullets. As the German reloaded, Charlotte grabbed her dagger and lunged at him. The *Boche* tried to block her with his rifle, but she was quicker. She thrust Pietro's blade deep into his heart. His knees buckled, and he fell. A startled look on his face.

Pulling her knife free, she returned to Théo. Crouching next to him, she took his hand. A weak smile crossed his lips. He whispered, *"Toujours."* His eyes glazed, and he was gone.

"No! I cannot lose you, too!" Charlotte cried, throwing herself over his body.

Jules ran to Charlotte. He pulled her up. "More Germans are coming," he yelled. *"Vite!"* She tried to wrench free, to stay with Théo, but Jules grabbed her around the waist and dragged her down the alley. He took her beyond the cobbles and into a dense cluster of oaks.

She sobbed, "I can't leave Théo."

Germans ran down a nearby alley. "Kill them all," yelled a soldier. "Those are the orders."

Jules whispered, "Théo's gone, Charlotte. There is nothing we can do for him."

"What about Rémi and the others?" she asked, choking on her tears.

"Rémi slipped into the trees, on the other side of the village. Marie was with him—maybe others." Jules took Charlotte's hand. "Follow me," he said, pulling her down a narrow rock-studded path.

***

Charlotte and Jules walked throughout the night, just as she and Rafael had done so many months before. Bands of soldiers rummaged through the woods, illuminating meadows with flashlights. Charlotte heard dogs, periodic gunfire, and screams.

Théo, she thought, wait for me. I don't think I will survive the night. We *will* be together again.

As morning light touched the surrounding

mountains, the two *maquisards* found refuge in a thicket of brush by a gentle stream.

"So thirsty," Charlotte gasped.

"Stay here," Jules said. "I'll get water."

Charlotte watched as he slid down the bank toward the river.

Just as Jules began filling his canteen, the trees rustled. Jules dodged into the brush as a German worked his way toward the muddy bank.

She retrieved her knife. Slowly, Charlotte took aim, but held back.

The soldier grunted as he came to a halt just short of the water. Dropping his pack, he pulled his canteen free and bent to fill it. Jules leapt on him from behind, pushing his head under water. The German thrashed about but the *maquisard* held him down until he drowned.

Charlotte watched Jules float the soldier's body and backpack into a clump of reeds—hiding it from soldiers that might follow.

She held her breath as Jules filled his canteen and rummaged through the German's pack, then made his way back up the slope. She stared at him blankly, tension and anxiety taking their toll.

Jules held the canteen to her lips. "Drink." She gulped the water down. "Now eat, then we'll move on." He handed her the German's bread.

She sat back on her haunches, ate, and listened. The rumble of planes overhead was constant. Charlotte watched as they flew in and out of surrounding valleys.

"They won't stop until they've killed us all." Charlotte's voice quavered.

"The *Boches* are searching for survivors in the grottos that dot the canyon walls," Jules said. "The caves and grottos are marked on all the local maps. I'm guessing *maquisards* have hidden in them. The Germans probably think the same."

"What can we do?" Charlotte asked, between bites of bread.

"Nothing. We can only hope our men have heard the planes and moved on."

"Look," Charlotte said, pointing high above them, on the canyon wall. "There's a woman in a white duster at the mouth of the cave. See? Just to the east of us, about two hundred meters."

"Must be the hospital Gaston set up. She's the doctor," Jules said, squinting. "I met her in Vassieux. A kind and gentle woman."

The crack of a twig broke the silence. Charlotte grabbed her dagger. A fox made its way to the river, seeking a morning drink.

"*Mon Dieu*," Charlotte whispered, clutching her chest. "I thought...."

"We were lucky. Now finish the bread and we'll move deeper into the woods."

Charlotte's body stiffened at the sharp staccato of rifle fire. "It's coming from the grotto—the hospital," she whispered. "The Germans must be killing the patients!" Horrified, she pressed her hand over her mouth. They watched as the soldiers took the doctor, shot her in the head, and threw her down the cliff.

"Burn in hell, you bastards. *Pallez au diable!*" Jules hissed.

"The *Boches*—they'll have no equal in hell."

She felt Jules take her hand. "Stay low," he said. "We need to get beyond the forest and down to one of the small villages, or we'll be next."

Chapter 32
Martyred in Vercors
July 15, 1944

Charlotte stumbled along a rough path that led away from Vassieux. Théo's glazed eyes haunted her.

Jules walked nearby, but they didn't speak. Nothing to say. The *Maquis* had failed. Their passion to make a difference and free France had overruled common sense.

Charlotte thought of *Flanders Fields,* a poem her father had recited. War will always be with us, she reminded herself. It haunted my father, now it haunts me.

"We are the dead . . .

To you from failing hands we throw the torch, be yours to hold it high . . ."

The words calmed her, soothed her grieving heart and the agony of losing her lover. He'd passed the torch to her and all the *maquisards.* Like the poem said, she must continue to fight—for him and for France.

Jules broke the silence. "There is a small farmhouse down there," he said, pointing through the trees. "Maybe the family can spare some food."

"Don't go," Charlotte pleaded. "The Germans may be hiding nearby, watching. Believe me. Please. I've seen this before. Everything looks safe, but it isn't. It could be a trap."

"Let me try," he said, stepping into the meadow that surrounded the small farm.

"No! It's not safe," she whispered into the air. But he'd already darted across the field and into the barn.

A deadly quiet surrounded her. *"Mon Dieu,"* she whispered. "Even the birds have stopped singing."

Charlotte crouched low, watching Jules move from barn to house. With every step he took, she expected gunfire. One more *maquisard*—dead.

Five minutes passed. What was taking so long? Then she saw him. Jules dashed from the house into the trees, working his way back to her.

"The husband and wife were very kind. They gave us food," Jules said, holding up a small packet. "Their son was in St-Michelle, another village in Vercors, when the Germans came. They're eager for news."

"What did you tell them?"

"I said it's possible their son survived and is hiding. Like us."

"Good. Now let's go. We're still too close to Vassieux," Charlotte said.

Before they could move, two German soldiers exited the trees from across the clearing, and walked toward the house. They didn't bother to knock. Kicking in the door, they stepped inside.

Charlotte shook her head as if waking from a stupor, and whispered to Jules. "The *Boches* will demand food, then kill them. We can't let that happen. Our guns are empty, but I have one blade left in my sheath. You use it. I have Pietro's dagger."

Adrenalin coursed through her body—a chance to kill two Germans filled her with renewed energy. She didn't fear for herself. She wanted vengeance—and she'd get it. Charlotte and Jules crouched low and ran for the house. "I see a back entrance. Follow me," she said.

Slipping into the house, they crept past the bedroom and halted just before entering the kitchen. Charlotte held up her hand. Jules pulled back. Peeking around the corner, she saw the Germans sitting at the kitchen table, eating soup and gobbling broth-soaked bread.

She signaled Jules to take the man closest to them. She'd put a stop to the other soldier's slurping.

Enjoy your last bite, she thought, as Jules flicked her knife at the German's temple. It cracked through bone and ripped into his brain. Blood spilled into his soup. He slumped onto the table, then slid to the floor— the knife still in his skull.

The other soldier gasped as his friend fell. The momentary pause was all she needed. Charlotte swept into the room, slashed the German's throat, and threw him on top of the first one. Blood pooled on the wooden floor.

The farmer's wife buried her head on her husband's chest, sobbing. He held her, glancing plaintively at Charlotte.

"Grab a coat and any food you can carry," Jules said. "We have to leave, immediately. More *Boches* are sure to follow, and they'll kill you if they see this."

Charlotte helped the woman gather clothing and a couple of blankets. Her husband packed food. Within minutes they were in the forest, heading toward Molières-Glandaz—the town Rémi suggested as a rendezvous if anything went wrong. And, alas, *everything* had gone wrong.

***

The four of them spent the night in the forest. Waking before sunrise, they ate quickly, and moved on. The couple guessed they were about four kilometers from Molières. "The brush is too thick," the husband said. "We'll have to walk along the edge of the road."

An hour passed. Dawn was breaking. Headlights advanced in the gray morning light. "A car is coming," Charlotte warned. "Over here, quickly." She pulled the woman into a ditch. Jules pushed the husband in, leaping in behind him.

Charlotte peeked over the berm—using weeds as a cover. "Nazis," she whispered. "No one else would drive a washed and polished convertible."

The car slowed down at a "Y" in the road. Charlotte guessed they were unfamiliar with the area— otherwise, why stop?

She ducked her head.

Charlotte heard "*Mach schnell!*" The car moved down the road. Then stopped again.

"Stay where you are," Jules whispered to the family. "I've heard about a trick they use. Luring us out in the open, thinking they've moved on, then shooting us down."

He was right. A couple of soldiers walked back to the intersection.

"No one here," the soldier said. "I'm not poking at trees in the forest. The *Generalmajor* is crazy. Tell him we didn't see anything."

Charlotte heard the men walk away, car doors open and close, and the auto continue down the road.

"Okay. Everyone out, and walk fast," Jules said, helping the husband and wife to their feet. "We should be in Molières by noon."

Village Molières-Glandaz

Charlotte was the first to see them. Rémi leaned against the stone wall of a café, smoking a cigarette. Marie hugged his arm, looking anxiously down the street.

Charlotte waved and ran ahead of Jules, falling into waiting arms.

"You made it!" Charlotte cried. "But where are Robin and Patrick?"

Rémi's voice caught, "Robin was killed at the beginning of the battle. A mortar hit a building near him. He was crushed under the rubble."

"*Mon Dieu,* another one of us," Jules said, shaking his head.

"And, Théo? What about Théo?" Marie asked.

Tears glistened in Charlotte's eyes and her lips trembled.

Jules answered. "Théo was killed, but he took *Boches* with him."

Charlotte wiped her eyes with the back of her hand, and took a deep breath. "And Patrick. Did he survive?"

Rémi interjected, "Let's step into the alley. Germans still patrol. We can talk there, quietly."

The group moved between the buildings, anxious to hear about Patrick.

"Patrick spent the first night with us in the forest," Marie said. "We were just below the large caves—the grottos high on the canyon walls. One cave was used as a makeshift hospital. Patrick decided to help them," Marie said.

"Oh no," Charlotte cried. "We saw Germans shoot the patients and medics. They shot the doctor, too. I suspect everyone was killed."

The farmer's wife gasped and began to cry.

"This talk is too much for my wife. Our son was in St-Michelle when the Germans attacked. He is only seventeen," the farmer sighed.

Charlotte took the woman's hand. "Rémi, Marie, these kind people gave us food. Jules and I feared for their lives, so we brought them here. We left two dead Germans in their home. They'll need a place to stay while they wait for news about their son."

"I have a room," Rémi said. "It's crowded, but you're welcome to join us."

The farmer shook his head. "My wife's sister lives here," he said. "We'll stay with her and wait for news."

July 16, Molières-Glandaz

Over lunch on the patio of a secluded café, Charlotte listened intently as Rémi explained why the British had abandoned them, leaving the *Maquis* open to massacre.

"Molières is lucky to have a wireless operator in the village. He changes location constantly, and reports what he's heard every evening. Villagers shared the information—filling us in on the Allied troops."

Charlotte leaned forward, anxious to hear the news.

"After they invaded Normandy, the armies began working their way toward Paris. The Allies met with more resistance than expected. Neither the British nor the Americans could spare any support for Vercors."

"We didn't need much, just some arms, medicine, and a few airplanes to bomb the German encampments. Was it too much to ask?" Charlotte said.

"I think the British hoped the French would take care of their own," Rémi said. "We discovered, only yesterday, that Resistance leaders met with de Gaulle in Algiers before D-Day. De Gaulle bragged about his army and air force. The leaders came away believing he'd support them in Vercors. But apparently he was in London on D-Day—not even on the front line with his so-called army."

"This doesn't make sense. Why would de Gaulle abandon us and not participate in D-Day? We are his people—his citizens." Charlotte shook her head. "Who is this man, and what are his motives?"

Rémi had more to share. "It seems de Gaulle will do anything to be the next president of France. If that's true, *his* troops, such as they are, must liberate Paris—or at least give the impression. De Gaulle had no time for us."

"So," Jules added, "politics and the liberation of Paris reduced us to nothing more than a moth buzzing around a small candle."

"Maybe we let our enthusiasm get in the way of reality. But I still believe Churchill led us on. The English must live with themselves," Rémi sighed, rubbing the back of his neck.

"What should we do now?" Charlotte asked. "France is still occupied. The war isn't over."

"We have a lot to do," Rémi said. "We're hearing more every day about a mid-August Allied assault from the south. We don't know where yet, but we'll find out soon enough."

"Let's go back to Nice, where we can make a difference. We need to do whatever we can to help the Allies chase the *Boches* from of our country—forever," Charlotte said. "Otherwise, Théo and the others gave their lives for nothing."

"In a few days we'll return," Rémi said, touching Charlotte's hand. "Our men will always be remembered for their bravery and patriotism. Someday their valor will be recognized by everyone, not just us."

"And as far as Patrick is concerned, there is still hope. His papers haven't arrived in *le bureau de poste*. So he may still be alive," Marie said. "That's a reason to wait."

Charlotte sighed. At times she wished she'd died with Théo. But Jules spared her that fate.

July 22, 1944
Moliéres

Charlotte worried. Still no sign of Patrick, and Rémi had decided to leave for Nice the next day. If Patrick showed up, the villagers were told to give him a message—*Return to Falicon.*

Charlotte woke before dawn and slipped out of the room and onto the village square. She wanted to sit quietly with her memories of Théo, one last time.

She walked to the edge of town, and sat down on a large boulder. From there she watched the sun rise on a new day. The mountains surrounding Vassieux seemed to undulate as light glided across them—one peak after another until it warmed the very rock on which she sat.

"Good-bye, Théo ... my love." He was part of her past now, not her future. She mourned the loss of their dreams. *Toujours* for them had been a very short time. She would always keep him in her heart, but when she left Molières she must leave him behind.

Charlotte stood and gazed once more up the road that led to the mountains. A motion caught her eye along the east side. Someone walked there—in the shadows. He limped badly, supported by a makeshift crutch.

"Patrick?" she called. "Is that you?"

He stopped and tipped his head to one side. "Charlotte?"

"*Oui, oui, c'est moi.*" She ran to him and took him in her arms. "We thought you were dead."

"And I thought the same of you," he said, smiling weakly.

Charlotte pulled his arm around her shoulders, helping support him. "We've been waiting, hoping you'd survived. We're staying in the village. What took you so long? What happened?"

"It is a long story. Let me tell it once to everyone. I've had little to eat and I'm very tired."

"I'll take you to a café—one we frequent. Marie, Jules, and Rémi will be there."

Entering the village square, she helped Patrick into the café. Charlotte squinted through the dim light. The *maquisards* sat at a table in the back of the room.

"Patrick!" Jules yelled, as they approached. "You made it! *Mon ami*, you *are* alive!"

Marie and Rémi hugged and kissed Patrick as Charlotte helped him to a seat. The room burst with applause.

"One more *maquisard* lives," Rémi said with a smile.

***

Charlotte and Marie took Patrick to their room, filled a tub with hot water, let him soak and wash, and gave him clean clothes. Marie took a look at the gash on his leg. It had begun to fester, making it painful to walk. She cleaned the wound, and wrapped it.

They rejoined their friends in a small park, off the village center. Patrick filled them in on his last days in Vercors.

"I was headed towards the makeshift hospital when I spotted Gaston and his family walking to Le Crest. I tried to discourage him—it's such a long way, but he was adamant. He said friends and family were there and he wanted to make certain his wife and son would be safe. Other *maquisards* were going there too, so I suspect he made it safely."

"But what happened to you?" Charlotte asked.

"I approached the hospital carefully, hiding behind trees and undergrowth. There was still a lot of fighting on the plateau. I was in the brush, just below the opening to the grotto, when Gestapo trucks pulled up. I curled up, hoping no one would see me. German soldiers jumped out, armed with rifles, and ran into the cave."

Charlotte gasped. "Jules and I were there—in the valley below the grotto."

Patrick nodded. "I heard the German commander order his men to kill everyone, even the doctor. 'Save bullets,' he said, telling them to strangle or bayonet anyone who couldn't resist, and shoot those who tried to escape. The screams were horrible."

"We heard them from below," Jules said.

"I stayed where I was for the rest of the day. That

night searchlights swept the area—Germans looking for anything or anyone still alive. My muscles ached and cramped, but I didn't dare move. In the morning the trucks and soldiers moved off. Only then did I discover a number of *maquisards* had hidden nearby. When night came we headed into the forest, away from the road. It's a good thing we did. The Germans returned with their big searchlights, again looking for survivors."

"The *Boches*—they never give up," Rémi said.

"The next day we buried the dead. In Vassieux, there were about two hundred *maquisards* and fifty or so women and children. We dug shallow graves, and covered them with dirt as quickly as we could. The smell...," Patrick rubbed his forehead, "was awful. I'll never forget."

"I'm so sorry," Charlotte said, touching his arm.

"But the worst thing...," he paused, shaking his head and drawing a sharp breath—"I buried Théo."

"*Mon Dieu*," Charlotte gasped. She'd hoped for a miracle. It wasn't rational. She'd seen Théo die. But hearing Patrick say he buried him finalized it in her mind. Her lover was gone, forever.

Chapter 33
Return to Falicon
July 28, 1944

Based on wireless reports, Rémi anticipated the Allied invasion on the Côte-d'Azur within a few weeks. "We have our assignment," he told his *maquisards* in their new house in Falicon. "De Gaulle's Free French Army is infiltrating the coast. They'll be our liaison with the Brits and Americans.

"The Allies have asked us to prepare up-to-date maps of the Riviera. They'll provide large basic maps of Provence—each one a section of the coast. We have to fill in the current condition of bridges, roads, and communication sites."

"Who better than us?" Jules said. "We're on the ground and we know what we've already sabotaged, especially the train lines. We'll also have a good idea where Germans might retreat and dig in—try to defeat the Allies."

"*Oui*," Rémi said. "They also want information on

river crossings that can handle large vehicles, and pastures where their troops can camp."

"Where do we get the maps?" Charlotte asked.

"They were dropped last night, in canisters with instructions for each of the *Maquis* cells. We'll retrieve ours today in Nice. Much of the work will be done right here on the kitchen table," Rémi said. "But we'll also need to do some scouting and wireless communication with *maquisards* in the area."

"What's our deadline?" Marie asked.

"That will be in the canisters. I suspect a week," Rémi said. "Jules and Charlotte, I'd like you to leave for Nice immediately. The pickup site is in the flower market on the edge of Old Nice. Be very careful. The Nazis are trying to intercept any communication between the Allies and *Maquis*."

***

By midafternoon Jules and Charlotte had returned to Falicon with the canister. They'd hidden it with vegetables and long-stemmed flowers—placing everything in a hefty cloth bag, just as they'd carried baguettes in peacetime.

Rémi pulled the maps out—leaving them rolled up on the table, as he read the instructions. "We have until August 6 to complete the maps. That gives us a week. We'll drop them off in Antibes, at Café Annette."

"Let's see what we're starting with," Patrick said.

"We have five maps." Rémi said, unrolling one. "Oversized, to leave room for notes, I'm guessing." He rolled the others out. "Overall attention to logistics is critical, for a very large army," Rémi said, distributing them. "There's one for each of us. Start filling in where you see the areas marked with large question marks. If you get stuck, call out."

The maps included the coastal area from Antibes to Menton, north to Vence, Eze, and La Turbie. Narrow and winding roads through the Maritime Alps didn't make a likely invasion route—but the Germans hadn't expected Normandy either—so anything was possible.

They worked individually until dinner. After the meal, they tacked their maps up on the kitchen wall and reviewed them together.

"Patrick," Jules said, pointing at his map, "the main bridge across the Var is gone. *Maquisards* replaced it with a footbridge. The Allies will have to rebuild to get tanks and supply trucks from one side to the other. You'll want to note that."

Patrick scribbled the information down, then looked at Charlotte's map. "Be sure to emphasize how narrow the roads are in Eze and La Turbie."

"Will do, but I'm wondering if the *Boches* will hide there, knowing the difficulty of maneuvering men and trucks up the roads," Charlotte said.

"The Germans might hide there, but I don't think they'd stay for long. They'll want to get to Italy as soon as possible," Rémi said.

"Let's not try to outguess the Germans or the Allies, or we'll be here all night," Marie said, yawning.

"Good point. And it looks like we need sleep," Rémi said. "We'll work on the maps in the morning."

Everyone had other responsibilities in addition to the maps—from preparing meals to picking up written messages in designated drops. Rémi worked with *Maquis* up and down the coast, to coordinate with de Gaulle's army. Small cadres of the Free French army slipped into France over the Pyrenees, and in boats along the coast.

Messages indicated 15,000 *maquisards* were gathering along the Riviera. If that was true, the Resistance was far larger than anyone imagined. Some men prepared to fight alongside the Allies, others were encouraged to wait until the Allies struck and moved north, then spread out behind them cleansing the smaller cities of the enemy. Rémi was content with the mapping assignment—having just lost two men in Vercors.

It took a week to gather all the necessary information. Meetings in cafés, wireless, and written notes contributed to the most reliable maps. Everyone tried to guess where the Allies might land. Most of the speculation suggested Cannes. It provided a large bay, flat ground, and was a midpoint between Nice and Marseille. By August 6, the maps were completed and dropped off in Antibes. The Free French collected and delivered them to the Allies, who waited in ships off the coast.

August 15, 1944
Falicon

"They're here at last!" Charlotte shouted. The *Maquis* heard the sounds of the invasion before dawn. The Allies had arrived. As the sun rose, villagers climbed atop roofs—watching and cheering the ships and planes. The beaches west of Nice were packed with boats off-loading men, tanks, and matériel. Planes swooped overhead, protecting the troops and bombing German communication centers. Black smoke from explosions was visible as far east as Falicon—a prime spot to view the invasion.

"They're not landing in Nice," Patrick said. "As expected, they're up the coast in Frejus and Cannes."

"Surely they'll move troops into Nice and then Italy. Soon both of my countries will be free!" Charlotte cheered.

"A glorious day!" Marie said, hugging Rémi.

***

Operation Dragoon, the name given to the Allied invasion, moved quickly inland, spreading north toward Lyon and west to Marseille. Most Germans retreated or immediately surrendered. But a few days after the Allies landed, wireless messages told another story. Some *Boches* refused to surrender, prolonging the inevitable and costing the Brits, Americans, and French precious time and lives in their movement north.

As the days passed and Allied troops moved farther inland, truth about the Gestapo's worst atrocities began to surface. The Falicon *Maquis* were horrified to learn that Marguerite, leader of the Cannes *Maquis*, had been brutally tortured only days before the invasion. The Gestapo had smashed her face, breaking her nose and cheekbones. They whipped her daily, and branded her face with swastikas. On August 15th, the day of the invasion, she was taken to an open field above Cannes, and shot dead.

Marguerite, the *Maquis* learned, was not the exception. The Gestapo, in an attempt to hide the worst of their atrocities, murdered many captives—dumping them into a common pit and hurriedly covering it over.

De Gaulle and the Allies liberated Paris on August 25th. No matter what the French felt about their new president, they realized he was the leader they needed—part military man and part politician. With an army at his disposal, he could pull the fragmented country together and rebuild France.

Falicon
August 26, 1944

Over an evening meal, the Falicon *Maquis* discussed their future.

"We should begin making plans. All of France will be liberated soon," Rémi said, optimistically.

"I have nowhere to go," Charlotte said. "I need time to plan."

"I think we should remain together," Patrick said, "at least until all of Europe is free. We'll have more choices then, more opportunities."

"Just because we believe France may be freed soon," Marie said, "doesn't solve the problem of food scarcity and housing. Like Charlotte, I want to stay here—at least until spring. We have a home."

"Alright, but what about food?" Rémi said.

"There are abandoned orchards nearby with fruit ready to drop," Charlotte said. "Some farms haven't seen their owners for years, but fruit and vegetables continue to thrive. We can combine squash, tomatoes, and cucumbers with rabbit and make...."

A chorus of moans filled the house.

"If I never eat another rabbit I'll be a happy man," Patrick laughed.

"The coming winter will be difficult if we don't prepare now," Charlotte said. "There are usually a few herbs for sale in the market in Old Nice. We can add those to the stew and pretend we're eating duck."

The room filled with laughter. Patrick smiled and shook his head.

"We'll can fruits and vegetables," Marie said, "but we'll need jars and paraffin."

"Why don't you and Jules buy what's needed in Nice? Everyone else ... rummage through abandoned homes," Rémi said. "I'll work on the old van, and will wait for you at the bottom of the hill, so you don't have to carry the jars up the hill to Falicon."

"But is it safe in Nice?" Charlotte asked. "I'm still worried."

"Just yesterday I heard the Gestapo had cleared out. If my information is good, and I believe it is, the *Boches* are running for their lives," Rémi said. "A lot has changed in a few days. There is nothing to fear. The Allies have landed," he said.

Chapter 34
Nice
August 27, 1944

The aroma of fresh coffee filled the air. Marie sat with Jules in a small café in Nice. She smiled, as she bit into a freshly baked croissant. "Let's stay here until the shops open. I want to soak up this glorious day—watch the sun rise over the bay."

"Freedom," Jules said. "That's what you're enjoying. I only wish Théo and Robin could be here, too."

Marie sighed. "I miss them terribly."

Jules paused before speaking—lost in memories. "Always soup and bread in the old farmhouse. That's all we had," he mumbled. "But it didn't matter. We were together."

Marie touched his sleeve. "The market is open. We should be on our way."

Before the war, the Nice market had a reputation

for beautiful flowers, luscious fruit, vegetables, and bread. Today the best products were family treasures that had been stashed in attics and basements during the Occupation. People needed money to purchase food—what little there was of it—so they scavenged their belongings and sold them in the open market.

The once elegant shopping stalls were now a large flea market.

"Over here," Marie called Jules. "There's a box filled with jars." They piled them into their bags, paid the proprietor, and moved on to purchase the paraffin.

"Oh, look! A full table of herbs and spices. Provence hasn't forgotten its sweet and savory cuisine," Marie said. "So, what do you want your rabbit to taste like? Rosemary? Thyme? Chives? Garlic?"

"Marie, you've never made anything I didn't like. You decide. Leave the bags with me. I'll wait here while you shop." Jules said, sitting on a wooden box. "The bottles will be heavy enough on our return to Falicon, especially if Rémi can't meet us in the van."

Before Marie could step away, she saw a man approach Jules from behind and tap him on the shoulder.

Jules turned. "Jean! I thought you were in Marseille. What are you doing here? Is Marseille liberated?"

"Today or tomorrow. When I left, the Allies were closing in," Jean said.

"Fantastic news!" Jules said. "But I forget my manners. Let me introduce you to Marie. Like me, she is a member of the Falicon *Maquis*."

Jean took Marie's hand, kissed it, and bowed slightly. "*Enchanté, mademoiselle.*"

She blushed. "My real name is Anna."

"It feels good to hear your real name again, doesn't it?" Jean said.

"*Oui*, it's wonderful. And I wish I could stay and talk, but I should finish shopping. You and Jules can chat for a bit."

Marie found a long table decorated with small baskets of spices and herbs. She picked herbs that would flavor a variety of meats and vegetables, and spices for baking. Toting up her purchases, she returned to the two men.

Smiling, she stooped to pick up one of the large bags. "Jules, you have a lot to share with your friend. Why don't you stay and talk a little longer? I'll start back, and you can catch up."

"I don't know," Jules said. "There are still some Germans...."

"I'll be fine," Marie said. "A few minutes won't hurt."

***

Jules watched as Marie worked her way through the crowd, then turned to Jean. "Please sit," he said pointing to a box. "I can't stay long."

"Someone special?" Jean asked, with a wink.

"Marie? *Non.* She's committed to a friend. You know Rémi ... err, Edouard Bonhomme?" Jules said.

"He is alive too? This *is* a good day," Jean said.

"Now tell me about yourself. Why are you in Nice when Marseille is so close to liberation?" Jules asked.

"I'm part of a small army of *maquisards*. There are about two hundred of us. We're cleansing the *Boches* from cities that the Allies skipped, like Nice and the hill towns. It's important we act quickly."

"Do you take Germans prisoner, or kill them on the spot," Jules asked.

"It's not pretty," Jean said. "You'll see soon enough. There will be hangings and mutilations. Nothing they didn't do to us, but I chose to run reconnaissance. I don't have the stomach for killing and torture."

"I'm surprised Edouard hasn't heard about this—shared it with us," Jules said.

"As the Allies moved on Marseille, all wireless was blocked," Jean said. "We couldn't send or receive and our mission came together quickly—over a couple of days.

"When we heard the Gestapo were murdering prisoners and dumping them in mass graves, we knew we needed to move fast if we wanted to catch them. Even if we could have contacted you, I doubt we'd have done so. Any contact with the towns and villages might have compromised us and put the *Boches* on alert. We're hoping to get to Menton in a few days, then head north and loop back among the hill towns, like Eze and Grasse. We don't want to simply chase the Germans from our land, we want to kill them."

"What can we do? We're just up the hill in

Falicon," Jules said.

"I'd suggest you remain there. Just stay out of the way. This band of Resistance fighters is pretty brutal. Vengeance often overcomes common sense."

"So exactly what are your responsibilities?" Jules asked.

"My job is to pinpoint remaining Germans, so when the *maquisards* enter Nice tomorrow they'll know right where to go. That's why I'm here today."

"Are there Gestapo still in Nice? We blew up their headquarters, you know. Thought the few remaining had left," Jules said.

"I've discovered some. Enough to bring our men here," Jean said.

Jules stood and grabbed his bags. "I need to catch up with Marie. What you've just told me …. She could be in grave danger."

"If I thought she might be threatened I'd have cautioned her, but the Germans we're searching for are holing up along the Promenade—in the old hotels. Don't worry," Jean said.

"I need to find her," Jules said, ignoring Jean. "I'll see you when France is liberated."

***

When Marie arrived at the Place de Garibaldi, on the northern edge of Nice, she glanced around hoping to see Rémi and his van. Her packages were getting heavy. But he wasn't there, and Jules hadn't caught up. Shrugging, she continued up the road.

Within minutes, Marie heard a car advancing from

behind. She glanced back to see a driver and two Germans in uniform, closing in.

Dropping her bags at the edge of the road, she fled into a thicket. What did they want? The war was over.

Bullets whizzed over her head. They were shooting! Trying to frighten or kill?

Marie crouched on all fours, pushing and crawling through the bushes. Brambles scratched her face and ripped her dress. Her breath came in short gasps.

More shots! A bullet sliced across her back, tearing through muscle and flesh. She screamed out in pain.

Digging her fingers into the dirt, she pulled herself forward, deeper into the undergrowth. Her back felt like fire—where the bullet ripped the flesh. She felt blood run down her side. Glancing back, she saw a large red stain growing on her dress.

Another vehicle, a van, came down the hill. She spotted it through the brush. Rémi was here! She listened as the van braked suddenly, and men jumped out. Guns fired. Someone yelled in German. Then more shots. A car skidded downhill—hitting something and coming to a stop.

Rémi called out, "Marie! Jules! Are you in there?"

"*Oui*," she gasped. "In the brush. I've been shot."

Chapter 35
We'll Meet Again
Cannes

Charlotte nursed Marie for three days. The bullet wound was festering—oozing pus. Each day that followed, Charlotte worried more. On the sixth day, Marie became delirious.

Charlotte pulled Rémi to Marie's bed. "Her wounds are getting worse, and her temperature reads thirty-eight degrees celsius. We need penicillin. Go to the Allied hospital in Cannes. Beg for it if you must. Without the medicine, Marie will die."

"I'll leave immediately," Rémi said.

"I'll do what I can while you're gone, but hurry."

Rémi kissed Marie on the cheek, then turned to Charlotte. "If I hadn't been so certain the Germans were gone.... I thought we were safe."

"You couldn't predict three drunk Germans looking to kill one more Frenchman. They're dead. You killed them. Now we must save Marie."

Marie's fever grew worse. She mumbled and tossed in delirium. Charlotte applied a cool towel to her friend's head, then checked the wound. Still festering. Charlotte wiped it clean, applied a poultice, and bandaged it.

Rémi hadn't returned. Every hour mattered. Charlotte worried Marie would die. She hung her head. "Please God, please don't take Marie."

Shortly before sunset, they heard a knock at the door.

Charlotte peeked through the curtains. "He's back."

Patrick opened the door and Rémi swept into the room. Charlotte sighed in relief. "Did you get the medicine?" she asked.

"Yes," Rémi said. "It wasn't easy, but when I told a doctor the Falicon *Maquis* prepared the maps for the Allies, he was very grateful and eager to help. "How is she?"

"The same," Charlotte said.

He drew in a deep breath. "Here's the medicine and a syringe. One dose daily. There's enough for three days. Can you give her the shots? I can't stop shaking."

"Could it be you haven't eaten?" Charlotte asked.

"There wasn't time," he said.

"Make time now, before you faint. There's cheese in the larder, and bread. Maybe a little wine will calm you." Charlotte took the syringe and vial from Rémi and turned to Patrick.

"I need your help," she told Patrick. "Marie is shaking and I need to give her a shot. Please hold her.

When I'm done, put the needle in a pan of boiling water. We'll have to use it again."

***

"It's taken a full day, but she's better," Charlotte said. "The infection has subsided."

"Thank God. What more can we do?" Rémi asked.

"Wait, and pray," Charlotte cautioned.

Rémi bent over the bed and kissed Marie. Her eyes fluttered open.

"Where am I?" she whispered.

"Here, in Falicon. You were shot," Charlotte said. "How do you feel?"

"Nauseated. My chest hurts, and my back burns ... but I'm hungry."

"I'll get some broth."

Charlotte warmed the broth, and poured it into a mug with a handle—something for Marie to grip.

"Let's prop her up," Rémi said.

Charlotte handed her the soup and cautioned, "Drink slowly. Small, careful sips are best for the stomach after days of just water."

"Thank you," Marie said between sips. "What happened to me? I don't remember much."

"You were shot by Germans," Rémi said. "But they won't be shooting anyone else."

"Good," she said, handing the mug back to Charlotte. "You killed them?"

Rémi nodded. "Now sleep. I'll be right here." He placed his hand on her wrist.

***

In the middle of the night Charlotte heard Rémi call. "Help! Charlotte! I need help!"

She jumped out of bed and ran to Marie's side.

"She's coughing and retching," Rémi said.

"Prop her up. It's the broth. She hadn't eaten in days," Charlotte said.

"But, there is more than broth," Rémi said. "There's blood."

"Oh, God, no. What's happening?"

Charlotte felt Marie's forehead. "She's burning up. The fever's back—worse than before."

Ten minutes passed before the coughing subsided. By then Marie was exhausted. "What's wrong with me?" she sobbed.

"Don't worry. We've given you penicillin. I'll get a cold towel to cool you down," Charlotte said.

When she returned, Marie was slumped back in bed. Her breathing—labored.

"Rémi," Charlotte said. "Come here." They stepped into the kitchen. "We need to take Marie to the hospital. They must take her. I'll wrap Marie in a blanket. Help me lift her into the back of the truck. I'll hold her. You drive."

***

Charlotte and Rémi arrived at the hospital soon after 3h00. An American soldier stopped them at the vehicle entrance. Rémi handed over their papers.

"Please. We're the Falicon *Maquis*. Germans shot Marie about a week ago. She's in the truck. One of your doctors gave us penicillin, but she hasn't gotten better.

We're afraid she'll die without your help," Rémi said.

"I'll check with the doctor on duty," the soldier said, picking up a phone and making a call.

"Okay, bring her to triage—to your left. A doctor will be waiting."

Once they were inside, a nurse took Marie's temperature and a doctor checked her wounds and lungs. "She has pneumonia," the doctor said, "and a very bad infection. We need to get her into a cold bath, to bring her temperature down. It's forty degrees."

Charlotte gasped. "She can't sustain it!"

The cool water succeeded in reducing her temperature by a few degrees. Nurses pulled her from the tub, dressed her wound, placed her in a bed, and propped her up with pillows.

There were no private rooms, but patients needing immediate attention had curtains between beds. The lights were dim throughout the ward to accommodate those who could sleep and those who required constant monitoring. The smell of antiseptic filled the air.

The doctor returned and took Marie's arm. "Penicillin." She barely flinched as the cold liquid flowed into her veins.

"I'll leave you with her. Let me know if there's a change for the worse."

"We will," Rémi said. "*Merci.*"

"This has to work," Charlotte whispered to Rémi.

"I know," he said, choking.

***

Just as the sun rose over the waters of the Riviera,

Rémi heard Marie call out.

He moved to her side and took her hand. Charlotte stood nearby.

In a barely audible voice Marie whispered, "I love you. Remember me." She paused and swallowed hard. "When the war is over—find Antonio."

She slipped into unconsciousness. Rémi sat next to her. Holding her hand. He was too afraid to leave her side.

An hour later Charlotte heard him cry, "Anna, no ... please don't...!"

But she was gone.

Chapter 36
Taking Back Our Names
Falicon

Catalina watched as they lowered Anna into the grave. The beauty of a warm summer evening in the heart of Provence was lost on the Falicon *Maquis*. They gathered just beyond the farmhouse, on the edge of the woods. Another friend and member of the *Maquis* family—dead.

"Anna gave her life for France. Like Hugo and Antoine (Théo and Robin), we must not forget her sacrifice." Edouard crossed himself and signaled the *maquisards* to complete the burial.

Only the sound of shovels in dirt and the soft warble of a Golden Oriole broke the silence.

Catalina bent to place a wooden cross and a single rose on the grave. The *Maquis* were reduced to four: Catalina, Edouard, Henri, and Gérard (Patrick and Jules). They stood, hugged each other tightly, grasped hands, and walked back to the farmhouse. As the sun set they gathered around a wood fire just outside the house.

Catalina sat quietly, remembering the first time she'd arrived in Falicon. Edouard Bonhomme, her childhood friend, had waited by a kerosene lamp as her blindfold was removed. He had welcomed her cautiously.

The *Maquis* eventually accepted her, but not before the train sabotage above the *calanque*, where they'd killed hundreds of German soldiers and destroyed a locomotive and its cars. So much had happened since then, it's a miracle *any* of us survived, she mused.

Edouard's hands shook as he poured each *maquisard* a glass of wine. "In memory of our loyal friends." He took a sip and set the glass down. Wiping tears from his face, he walked away from the group, and slipped into the trees.

Catalina ran after him. Taking Edouard into her arms, she heard him sob, "Anna was the love of my life. I never imagined losing her. Not now. Not after the Allied invasions. I tried to protect her."

Choked with tears, Catalina said, "I know. She was my sister, my *Maquis* sister. Now I've lost her and Hugo too. This war," she cried, "is so cruel."

"I will never love another woman—not like I loved Anna." Edouard shook his head. "Never."

"She would want you to love again," Catalina said. But Edouard didn't answer.

Drying their tears, they walked back to the farmhouse hand-in-hand.

***

Henri and Gerard sat near the fire—in a place where they'd often gathered. Only after a second glass did the *Maquis* begin to talk.

"Edouard," Catalina asked tentatively, "who is Antonio?"

Henri and Gérard looked up—curious.

"Anna's brother. He was in the north, just outside Paris, when the Germans invaded. He ended up in a forced labor camp in Alsace. His job was removing mines planted by our own soldiers. They'd hoped to block or delay the German invasion," Edouard sighed. "Little good it did. We heard during the height of the war Germans often forced their prisoners to walk across minefields, tripping the mechanisms. That's how they cleared a minefield for troop movement. Barbaric."

"Why didn't Anna tell us about him? She said her parents were killed and we were her only family," Catalina said

"She only told me," Edouard said. "Anna wanted to keep her brother's identity secret—especially when she joined the *Maquis*. It would have been deadly for both if she was caught and the association made. Brother and sister, both Resistance fighters." He shook his head. "It's been nearly three years since Antonio was taken, and we've heard nothing. Most likely he cleared a minefield with his life."

"The Allies may find him as they push into Germany," Catalina said.

"It's possible. If he's alive, I suspect he'll come searching for Anna and his parents. They lived in Nice, you remember." Edouard shook his head.

"It must have been awful for Anna—discovering her parents were dead and her brother held prisoner by the Germans," Catalina said. "I remember when you told me *my* parents were murdered. At that moment, I realized the *Maquis* were my family. The four of us that remain," she mused, "will be friends for life."

Catalina sat on the ground. Leaning back against a large rock, she sipped her wine, and glanced across the fire at Henri and Gérard. "I've just learned your real names. I feel like we're all exiting from a dark cave. We've been someone else, for years. Hiding from the Germans. I've heard your first names, but not your last."

"I am Henri Mirabeau," he said bowing slightly.

"And, Jules, uh, Gérard?" she asked.

"Gérard Le Monde, at your service," he said tipping his cap.

Catalina began to laugh. "We are meeting each other for the first time!" She stood, walked over to the men—hugged and kissed each one.

Smiling, she stood and asked, "Another glass of wine?"

"*Oui!*" they cried in unison.

"I'll get it. Bread and cheese," she said, stepping into the farmhouse. "There is nothing like a little wine to help us through our sorrows."

***

Within a few months, Catalina began to see more and more French citizens come out of hiding. They were taking back their homes in Nice and the surrounding villages. Many had to rebuild, as residences and businesses were in disrepair, or destroyed. But energy was in the air, as people reclaimed what was theirs.

The Falicon *Maquis* kept busy. Edouard moved his parents back to their apartment in the Russian quarter. Henri found work in a restaurant. Gérard joined the Nice gendarmerie. Catalina worked with the local farmers, helping them secure seeds and plants that would one day generate fruit and vegetables for the Nice market.

Through all of this change, the Falicon *Maquis* continued to live in the farmhouse. They planned to remain there until the owners returned—*if* they returned. The *maquisards* spent many nights discussing plans for the future. They had the opportunity to refocus their lives and live out their dreams.

"Will you return to Italy?" Edouard asked Catalina, one evening after dinner.

"No," she said. "There's nothing for me in Torino. My parents and Pietro are gone. The house was burned and the vineyards destroyed."

"But the land is still there. The village will rebuild," Henri said. "You could replant the vines and become a vintner, like your father."

"Perhaps I will become a vintner, but not in Italy. My father often spoke of California and the wineries north of San Francisco. He thought about starting anew there, but said time had passed him by for such adventures. Maybe I will follow his dream, take some cuttings of French and Italian vines, and travel to

California to start my own winery," she said.

"How could you afford to purchase land in California?" Edouard asked.

"Have you forgotten the blue diamond necklace?" she said.

"*Mon Dieu*, of course. But it's a family heirloom. Could you stand to part with it?" Edouard asked.

"A few days ago, I spoke with the chairman of *Banque Nice*. He told me that banks in America would allow customers to exchange what he called 'collateral' for a given amount of time, in exchange for cash. The necklace could serve as collateral—just to get started. When I earn enough money from the vineyard, I return what I borrowed and they'll give me the necklace."

"But is it still in the cave?" Edouard asked.

"I retrieved it a few days ago and placed it in a safe deposit box in the bank. It's secure for now—until I leave for America. I need to earn some money for travel, so don't worry. I won't be leaving for a while." Catalina smiled.

"But what are *your* plans," she asked the men. "Henri, have you thought about your future?"

"Yes, of course. Ever since I was very young, I wanted to own a restaurant in Paris. I'll start small, with a café, then move to a bistro on the Left Bank."

"And will Gertrude Stein be invited to your café?" Gérard asked.

"But of course, and her gaggle of artists and writers too!" Henri declared.

"I love your dream," Catalina said. "But I must

ask—will you serve *lapin*?"

They all burst out laughing.

"No rabbit will cross the threshold of my bistro! I will run it off with a broom, even if it sniffs at the door. I have my pride," he said, grinning.

Edouard yawned. "It has been a long day. I propose we save Gérard's plans and mine for another day. Mine are still evolving. But I assure you, they will be equal to *your* dreams."

Chapter 37
The Future is Ours
Falicon

January, 1945

Alone in the farmhouse, Catalina spent afternoons reading about grape varieties and winemaking. She took detailed notes, planning which vines she'd grow in California. Her father raised the rich aromatic Syrah grapes, and Catalina loved the red wine it produced. But she wanted more varieties to complement the Syrah.

As she leaned back in her chair mulling ideas, there was a sharp knock at the front door. Instinctively, she reached for her dagger, moved to the back door, exited, and slipped into the trees. Heart pounding, she crept around the house to the front. A tall thin man, dressed in shabby ill-fitting clothes, stood with his back to her. He knocked again.

Catalina moved behind him. Silently and quickly she grabbed him by the hair, pulled his head back, and pressed the blade to his throat.

"Who are you and why are you here?" she demanded.

"Antonio de Frabrizzio." Catalina felt him swallow. "I'm searching for my sister, Anna."

Catalina pulled her knife away from his throat. Drawing in a deep breath, she released him and stepped back beyond his range. "Show me your papers."

He turned around slowly. Digging into his coat pocket, he retrieved his identification and handed it to Catalina. "This is all I have. I've been in a German work camp for the past three years. We were released a month ago. I came home—searching for my family in Nice. Just yesterday, I learned my parents were killed."

Catalina glanced at his papers. The photo was of the same person. Black hair, hollow cheeks, and deeply set eyes. Sorrow etched his face. The poor man must have suffered terribly during the war. He was lucky to be alive.

"Do you know where my sister is? Her name is Anna. Someone in Nice suggested I come to Falicon. They said she's a member of the *Maquis*."

Catalina handed the man's papers back, and placed the knife in its sheath. "Sorry. Wartime habits are hard to break. The *maquisards* do live here. Please come in. I'll make tea. The others will be back soon. They'll want to meet you."

Taking time to brew the tea, Catalina wondered how she could tell Antonio that his sister was dead. More terrible news for this sad young man. She thought of how awful she'd felt when she learned of her own parent's deaths.

"Sit. We can talk here." She pointed to the kitchen table and poured him a cup of tea.

Catalina sat across from him and took a deep breath. "I'm sorry, Antonio, but I don't have good news. Anna was a member of the Falicon *Maquis*, but she was killed late last summer. Nazis."

His shoulders slumped. Resting his elbows on the table, he rubbed his face. "I was afraid of this," he said quietly. "She was so delicate.... Every day I prayed I'd see my family again. That kept me alive. Because of them, I never gave up." Antonio's voice caught. "Now, to learn they are all dead...."

He paused and stared out the window. "If I hadn't survived, my entire family would have been lost. Is this consolation? To continue the family name?" he asked, turning to Catalina.

She reached across the table and took his hand. The pain in his eyes was mirrored in hers. She knew his grief. "I'm so sorry," she said. "I loved Anna very much. She was like a sister. My parents and brother were also killed. Like you, I was orphaned by the war.

"This dagger," she held it out, "is all I have left of my family. I killed the *Boche* with it. It was the third knife in my small arsenal. I sought vengeance, and I found it—but it's time to let it go." She walked to the hearth and placed the knife on the mantle.

"The Falicon *Maquis* took me in," she said, walking back to the table. "Without them I don't know what I would have done." She took Antonio's hand and gave it a little squeeze. "You are welcome to stay here with us. We are family."

March, 1945

Catalina often found herself observing Antonio. Color returned to his cheeks and he put on weight. The creases that lined his face faded. He helped with daily chores and partnered with the *maquisards* in their daytime jobs. Like the others, he searched for a postwar mission.

"Do you know about growing grapes?" Catalina asked one afternoon.

"No. My parents grew vegetables and berries, but not grapes. We bought our wine in the Nice market."

"Would you like to learn? I have some books, and the small vineyards nearby are starting up again. I plan to visit some tomorrow. You can join me if you'd like."

"*Oui*, to both your questions. I like the idea of growing something, and working in the fields."

"*Bon*," Catalina said. "We'll visit three vineyards. Each grows a different grape. The leaves are just beginning to sprout on the vines. Maybe you can guess the grape they'll produce by identifying the leaves. Look through the books, so you'll be ready," she challenged.

He gazed at her as though studying a painting. Catalina blushed. She pulled out one of her books and placed it on the table. "Look at this one first. You'll see a difference in the leaves and the woody vines. And tomorrow, no fair asking the farmer what grape he is growing. You should know." She winked and went back to preparing dinner.

They started out early, while fog still laced the valleys that surrounded Falicon. It was a six-kilometer walk along a well-worn path to the first vineyard. As they mounted the crest of a hill, Catalina stopped to take in the view.

"Look down at the bay," she pointed. "The colors are beautiful. The water is, well, at least three shades of blue." Catalina turned and smiled at Antonio. "I don't think I could ever live far from the sea. It's breathtaking, *oui*?"

"And peaceful," Antonio said. "Do we have time to sit and talk?"

"Yes, of course."

"Ever since you said Anna was killed, I've wondered how it happened. Can you tell me?" Antonio asked.

Catalina looked out at Nice and the beautiful bay. She sighed with the heaviness of Anna's death. "It was just after the Allied invasion. Last August. The armies swept through the coastal cities very quickly. Their major objective—cut a swath north to the D-Day armies—meet up with them Paris. The suddenness of the Allied armies hitting the beaches and barreling forward drove many *Boches* into hiding. It also emboldened other Germans who dismissed the strength of the Allies."

"And so you came out of hiding too soon?"

Antonio asked.

"Yes. Only a few days too soon, but...."

"But just enough for the last Germans to kill a few more French." Antonio said, shaking his head.

"Yes. Anna walked to Nice to make some purchases. On the way home a carload of Nazis shot and killed her. Edouard arrived in time to kill the Germans—every last one of them." She thought that was enough information. She didn't want Antonio to blame Edouard or Jules for Anna's death, and she didn't want him to dwell on Anna's last days.

"Timing," Antonio mumbled. "Anna died because of timing, and I lived because of it."

"What do you mean?" Catalina asked.

"The German work camps in Alsace focused on disarming or detonating mines. Most of the time French captives were used to clear the mines. Their death was quick, if that's any consolation," Antonio said. "I was scheduled to walk the minefields the next day, when a German officer who'd just arrived at the camp asked if I could repair some wiring in his confiscated home. I knew enough to do the job, and from then on my captors called on me to repair anything electrical. So I lived, but many of my friends didn't."

Catalina took him in her arms and hugged the gentle soul who'd survived those agonizing three years. "Oh, Antonio, I am so glad you survived and came here to live with us." Her eyes glistened as she drew back—stroking his cheek.

Antonio moved toward her, ever so slowly, until

his lips met hers and the heat she'd known before filled her once again.

"I could stay right here, all day," she said softly, "but we must go. The vintners are expecting us."

Antonio stood, bent, and pulled Catalina up. She slipped her hand into his, as they gazed for a few moments at the rebuilding projects that dotted the landscape.

"I'm sure you couldn't have stood like this, out in the open, when France was occupied," Antonio said.

"No, we would have dropped down on all fours, just below the crest, and wiggled on our bellies to the top, poking our heads over the hill to look down into the valley."

Antonio laughed and shook his head.

"What's so funny?" Catalina asked.

He smiled. "The thought of you wiggling through the grass."

Another flash of heat went through her. She jutted her chin out and sassed back, "Now, follow me— upright, and on two feet."

They slipped over the crest and down the hill to a vintner's home. He worked in the yard while two young children chased each other around an old rusted truck.

"Catalina, it's good to see you. And this time you bring a friend," the vintner said, reaching out to shake hands.

"This is our new *maquisard*, Antonio. He joined us a few months ago," Catalina said.

"A new *maquisard*? The war is nearly over," the

farmer said.

"It's a bit of a story," Catalina said, glancing up at Antonio. "Another time."

"Ah, I undersand. So, tell me," the farmer said looking at Antonio, "are you interested in growing wine, like Catalina?"

"Perhaps. Right now, I'm here to learn," Antonio said.

"Well then, follow me." The farmer walked them to a small vineyard next to his house. "It's not large, but it will grow in size. I have more land."

Antonio studied the vines—brown, woody, and frayed. "No leaves yet?" he asked.

"Oh, no," the farmer said. "Those won't sprout for another month—and then they will burst out all at once! Like magic! A marvel to see."

Catalina felt Antonio's glance, but refused to let him catch her eye. He'd have questions later.

She gazed at the long rows of vines. The well-trained stalks stood ready to send shoots in every direction across the wires that linked the posts. She reached down and took a handful of the crumbled rocky soil. "This is ideal for growing the red *Braquet* grape, but didn't you say you were also growing *Grenache Blanc*?"

"You have a good eye, *mademoiselle*. The *Grenache* grows about a hundred meters south in a sandy loam. It's hard to believe the soil changes so quickly, but that's what makes the Provençal wines so enjoyable. We're famous for variety.

"We also love our *rosé,* especially on a warm summer afternoon," the farmer said, with a wink.

"Is there a percentage of red to white, and which grapes are used to blend your *rosé*?" Antonio asked.

"The *rosés* are our artist's palate. We are forever experimenting. It's like soup—slightly different every time," the vintner said, kissing the tips of his fingers.

"Do you think the *appellation* will require specific grapes and ratios sometime in the future?" Catalina asked.

"But of course," he said, shrugging and raising his hands in the air. "Until then, we experiment. And maybe afterwards too," he said, with a twinkle in his eye.

Each vintner they visited had something new to share. One spoke about harvesting—when the time was right and how they accomplished picking within a twenty-four hour period. Another discussed how to prune and "put the beds to rest" in the fall. All the farmers shared their techniques for making wine, adding that it was as much an art as a science.

By midafternoon, Catalina and Antonio were on their way home—back over the rolling green hills.

Antonio asked, "Did you know the leaves wouldn't be on the vines for at least another month?"

Catalina smiled. "Yes, I knew, but I was putting you to a little test. I wanted to see how serious you were about viticulture."

"So I demonstrated earnestness in learning and ignorance at the same time?"

"*Oui,*" she said, giggling.

"Okay. Now I have a test for you," he said.

"*S'il vous plaît*," Catalina said, wondering what he'd ask.

"How long would it take for you to snake your way to the top of that knoll?" He pointed off to the left.

"About five minutes," she said proudly.

"Shall we race?" he asked.

"*Certainement*," she said dropping to the ground and slithering toward the top of the hill.

She was on her stomach for about five meters, when she stopped to see how far behind she'd left Antonio.

He hadn't moved an inch. He was on his back in the grass, gripping his sides, laughing.

"You tricked me!" Catalina yelled, running back down the hill. He caught her just before she smacked him with her *musette*. Pulling her down into the grass, he rolled around with her until they were both giggling and gasping for air.

Finally coming to a stop, Antonio rested on one elbow and gazed down at Catalina. She reached up, her hand clasping the back of his neck, and pulled him down—welcoming his warm kiss.

He pulled back and cupped her face with his hand. "You are the woman I dreamed of, for three long years. How is it that I found you when I needed you the most?"

"Some things have no answer," she whispered, kissing him again.

***

"Look what I purchased today," Edouard said as he entered the farmhouse holding up a radio. "We can listen to news from London and Paris. The Allies are close to victory. It will be good to hear the voices of Churchill and de Gaulle."

"Victory is close" Catalina said. "I can feel the energy already."

Edouard plugged in the radio and began to move the dial. "The reception isn't good," he said. "We'll have to turn the antennae."

"Let me help," Antonio said. "I know a little about wiring."

Catalina glanced up, but said nothing.

The men attached bits of paper and cloth to the antennae—seeking the best reception. Edouard fiddled with the knobs as Antonio made adjustments. Finally, they arrived at the best combination, and set the radio for BBC.

"Okay, men, dinner is served," Catalina called.

Conversation quieted while they enjoyed *coq au vin* and *pain ordinaire*.

"This is delicious," Henri said. "Perhaps you should give up your dream of raising grapes and join me in Paris."

Antonio glanced at Henri, then Catalina. She'd felt his glance before. Was he jealous?

"I'm determined to build my vineyard in California. You can import my wine for your bistro, if you'd like," she said, laughing.

"Perhaps I will, but I think that would be a first.

Can you imagine American wine on Parisian tables?" Henri asked.

Catalina met Antonio's gaze. "Just you wait. California wines will be the envy of the world."

Everyone laughed. "If anyone can do it, Catalina can!" Edouard said.

Antonio tipped his head, and looked at Edouard. "I've seen you writing letters lately. Do they have anything to do with your plans for the future?"

"Yes. I've held off sharing until I was certain. I've decided to continue studying economics."

"If I remember you were a good two years into your degree," Gérard said.

"Yes, and now I have a real purpose," Edouard said. "Our nation—and all of Europe need to rebuild. Maybe I can work in government, once I graduate. I've sent my application to the Sorbonne. They've reopened the university now that the Germans are gone. I plan to be among the first students, come fall."

"This is fabulous news," Henri said. "Perhaps you and I can share an apartment—somewhere near Boulevard St-Germain."

"Perfect. Classes begin in September. Will you be ready?" Edouard asked.

"Of course," Henri said, lifting his glass of wine. "*Santé*. A toast to Edouard and his studies at the Sorbonne!"

The sound of clinking glass filled the room.

"Gérard," Catalina said. "Knowing that you were already working at the *gendarmerie*, we neglected to ask about your plans."

"Oh, my goals are simple. I'll remain a *gendarme,* for awhile. Using the skills I learned as a *maquisard*, I plan to become a detective." Gérard looked down at his plate, tore off a piece of bread, and sopped up the juices.

"Don't laugh," he said, popping the bread in his mouth. "Someday I'll work for the wealthy who live on Cap Ferrat. I'll help protect their big homes, fine art, and jewels."

"Gérard. Savior of the rich!" Henri said, holding up his glass.

"This is a fine dream," Catalina said, smiling.

"And take note, those who care for the wealthy often become rich too," Edouard said. "So, that's why you chose 'Jules' as your *nom de guerre*. It sounds like the English word—'jewels'."

Gérard laughed. "My little secret."

Catalina glanced across the table at Antonio. He was quiet, but a smile graced his lips. He enjoyed the *repartie*. Perhaps he will join me in California, she thought, biting her lip. Was that too much to hope?

May 7, 1945
Freedom

Germany surrendered unconditionally to the Allied powers on May 5, 1945. The announcement came over the radio several days in advance of the formal signing of papers on May 7 in Reims, France.

Charlotte and Antonio stood together in the Place de Medine, in the heart of Nice. The Resistance flag was draped from every window, and hung from every flagpole. Young men, long hunted by the Nazis, ran through the streets waving the flag and cheering.

The square was packed with revelers. Music filled the air. Fireworks arched over the surrounding gardens and ponds. There was no holding back. People sang, shouted, kissed, cried, and hugged.

"I am so happy, Antonio," Catalina yelled above the crowd. "Hold your ears. I'm going to scream!"

He laughed as her cheers filled the air.

At 22h00 the church bells rang from Nice to Eze, and north to Cimez. Singing of the *Marseillaise* followed, along with more cheering and fireworks.

Antonio folded his arms around Catalina and pulled her close. Their kisses had become more frequent since the first ones on the mountain, but this time she felt something different. There was a deeper passion. People bumped her from all sides, but Catalina ignored them. She was comfortable in his arms, and didn't want him to let her go—ever.

He bent over and brushed the hair from her face. "I love you, Catalina. Will you marry me?"

"*Oui!* But you must come to America," she said, cupping her hands around his ear.

"Of course! We'll raise juicy grapes and plump little babies!" he said, lifting her up and swinging her around.

"Do you think there's a bottle of champagne left in Nice?" she asked, laughing. "We need to share this news with our brothers!"

"Perhaps not in Nice, but there are two bottles in Falicon."

"Ah! You planned this?" she yelled.

He smiled. "But of course!"

***

Sunrise found the *maquisards* asleep in chairs and on the floor of the old farmhouse in Falicon. Wrapped in blankets, they'd camped out together for what could be the last time. Their stomachs full—very full—and their heads foggy with drink.

Catalina and Antonio snuggled in front of the fireplace, wrapped in each other's arms. She'd realized months ago that she couldn't compare him to Hugo, her dear Théo, who was buried in Vercors. Her first love was filled with passion, vengeance, and the horrible scars of war.

Her love for Antonio spoke of the future—a new nation, a lifetime of making wine, a family of their own. This was a love that would endure and sustain.

She pulled back, gazing at Antonio with softly hooded eyes, and whispered "*Je t'aime. Mon amour.* I will love you forever."

The Third Knife

Nom de Guerre	Character's Real Name	Role
Rémi Montagne	Edouard Bonhomme	*maquisard*
Charlotte Beaumont	Catalina Settevendemie	*maquisard*
Robin Roux	Antoine Rossin	*maquisard*
Patrick Hollande	Henri Mirabeau	*maquisard*
Jules Belanger	Gérard Le Monde	*maquisard*
Marie Leclair	Anna de Frabrizzio	*maquisard*
Théo Moreau	Hugo Girard	*maquisard*
The Hunter	Major Ulrich Jaeger	Gestapo commander
The White Fox	Elena Taylor	*Maquis* organizer

Characters without a *Nom de Guerre*

Antonio de Frabrizzio	Anna's brother/prisoner
Lorenzo	Italian military officer
Rafael	Catalina's guide
Nico Settevendemie	Catalina's father
Adelle Settevendemie	Catalina's mother
Pietro Settevendemie	Catalina's brother
Aunt [*zia*] Francine	Catalina's aunt

Note: The French *Maquis* (*maquisards*) were the resistance fighters in the countryside – primarily in southern France, during WWII. They were known for their sabotage of German trains, troops, munitions, and communications.

The following are maps and photographs that support and enrich the *The Third Knife.*

WWII Occupied France

For those who are not viewing this map in color, Savoy and Nice were annexed by Italy in 1942. Germany annexed Alsace/Lorraine in 1940.Vichy France, Savoy, and Nice were occupied by Germany in 1943, after Italy capitulated to the Allies.

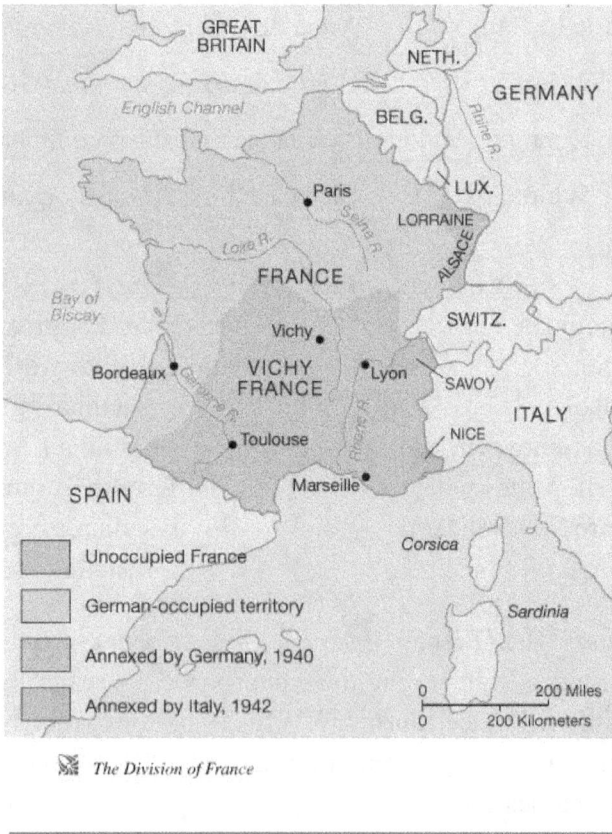

The Division of France

Europe and North Africa at the height of German Domination
1941 - 1942

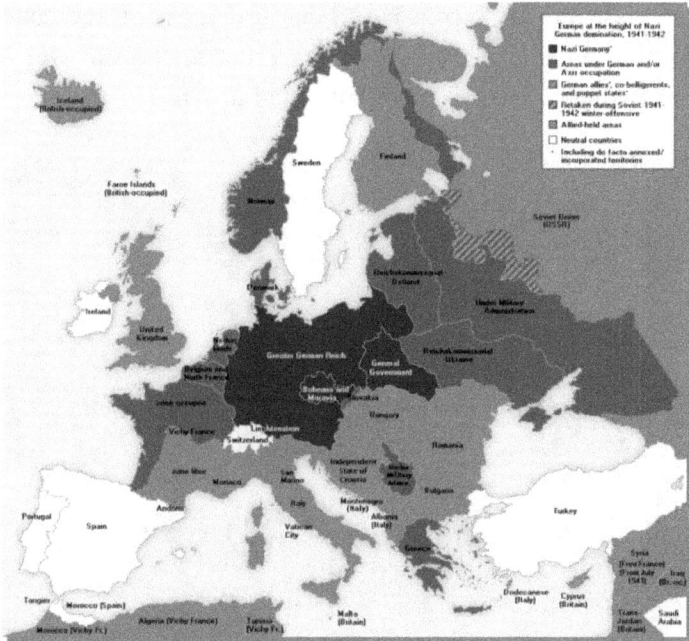

Map of the French Riviera, including Nice and Falicon.

See Falicon directly north of Nice.

Also see Cap Ferrat peninsula and St-Hospice on the tip of St-Jean-Cap Ferrat. Beaulieu-sur-Mer is on the coast – on the right of the peninsula. Villefranche-sur-Mer is on the left. These sites are all noted in *The Third Knife*.

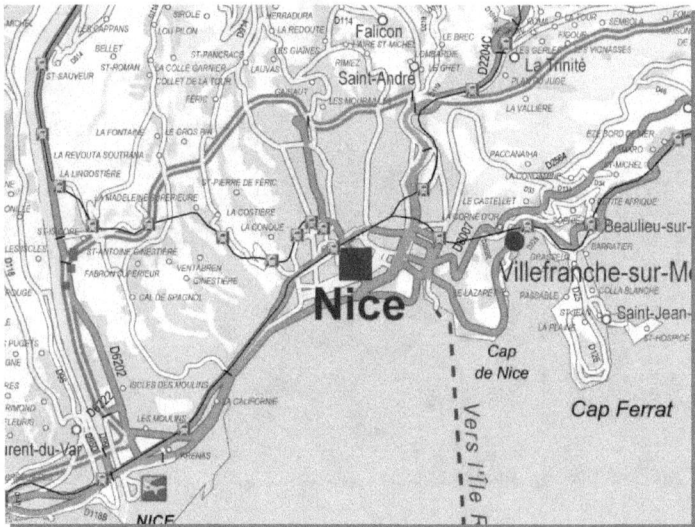

The French Maritime Alps, and Riviera

Catalina/Charlotte walked from Torino (just to the east of Col de Tende), south to Menton (on the coast), and west to Nice and Falicon.

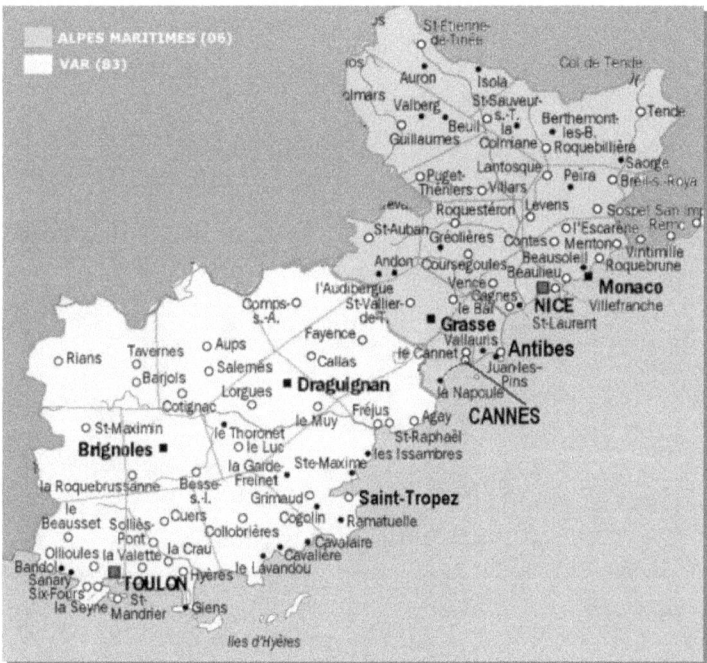

Vercors massif

The dot marks the location of plateaus, mountains, and villages of Vercors.

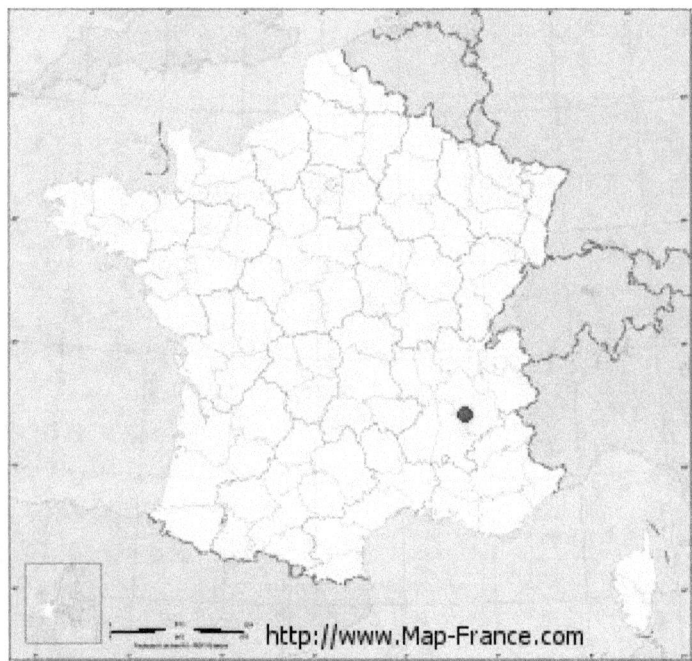

http://www.Map-France.com

View of Camaloc village—deep in the valley. A typical community within the Vercors massif.

The Lysander
"A Greek Bearing Gifts"

2015 Map of Europe

Pamela Boles Eglinski

Pamela Eglinski was born in San Francisco, and raised on the Peninsula. She holds a Master's degree in Asian Art History from the University of Kansas, and two masters degrees from Colorado State University – one in Asian/ European comparative history, and a second in Student Personnel Management & Counseling. Much of her career was spent in non-profit management. Pamela is the author of three novels in the *Catalina and Bonhomme Spy Series. **The Third Knife** is the prequel to **Return of the French Blue** and **She Rides with Genghis Khan.***

The Third Knife is a tale of espionage and heroism in the French Resistance. *Return of the French Blue* features the offspring of characters in *The Third Knife,* who take on the dark world of global terrorism.

Code Name: Purple Fire is Eglinski's first novella in a Special Ops series featuring CIA agent Abigail Scott, and SEAL team commander Cooper Sinclair. *Code Name: Yellow Fire,* and *Code Name: Crimson Fire* will be published in 2016.

Please enjoy Pamela's suspense-packed novels and novellas—based on historical fact laced with legends from the past. Eglinski entertains her readers, takes them to places rarely seen, and engages them in missions they never before imagined.

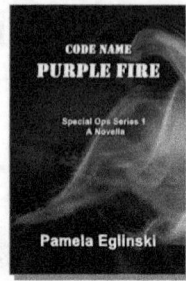

Click on a book cover above and go to Amazon where you can purchase either Kindle or paperback editions. When you have read the books, please leave a thoughtful review. Thank you, and watch for more suspense-packed novels and gripping novellas by Pamela Boles Eglinski.

Amazon Author Central: www.amazon.com/Pamela-Boles-Eglinski/e/B007GORNJ4

Facebook: www.facebook.com/pamela.b.eglinski.fans

Website: www.pamelaboleseglinski.com

Please enjoy an excerpt from the second novel in the Catalina & Bonhomme International Spy series, *Return of the French Blue*. It is set in contemporary times and introduces the offspring of Charlotte and Rémi.

RETURN OF THE FRENCH BLUE

Two diamond heists, two centuries
apart, history retold

PAMELA BOLES EGLINSKI

Chapter 1
Blue Stones Vineyard
Napa Valley, California 2012

It was a burglar's delight.

Once a year, the vintners of Napa Valley welcomed wealthy patrons to their private homes. The occasion: celebrate the bounty of California's wine country and raise millions of dollars to help the poor. Reputations were at stake and wine sales at risk. At $2,500 a ticket, everything must be perfect.

Catalina checked last-minute details. The family villa was festooned with tiny white lights. On the expansive patio, small round tables were covered with linen tablecloths and set with fine china and gold-rimmed crystal goblets. Lucas and Christiane Syrah, Catalina's parents and owners of Blue Stones Vineyard, anxiously awaited sixty dinner guests.

Catalina, or 'Cat' as she was known to family and friends, delivered orders like a police sergeant. But, unlike most sergeants, she was spectacularly gorgeous.

A blend of French and Italian ancestors, her eyes were dark and large, skin rosy pink and hair the color of ebony. Tall and thin, she raised eyebrows wherever she went.

"Sam!"

The head caterer jerked to attention.

"Make certain the bars are well stocked with the '94 Syrah and a good selection of liquor, and don't forget the ice."

"Got it covered, Ms. Syrah."

"And what about the centerpieces? I don't see the flowers yet."

"They just arrived. Here they come now, straight from the florist."

Cat glanced over her shoulder to see a parade of Japanese iris, mixed with polished greenery, making its way to the tables. The deep blue color was emblematic of the vineyard.

"Gorgeous," she whispered. Then the sergeant returned. "The food, the wine, the lights, the flowers." She was ticking them off on her fingers as she moved about the patio.

"Flip the switch on, Sam. I'd like to see the lights. I want to get a sense of the ambiance."

"Yes, ma'am."

"Ah," said Cat, "we need another string of lights around the base of the white oak. Can you do that? Just a small string."

"Of course. I'll do it immediately."

"And don't forget about the background music. I

want the stack of CDs next to the player, playing throughout dinner. They are all 1980s songs. That is our theme for the night. Be sure to have someone ready to place *Graceland* on the CD player just before I begin to dance. I want 'Diamonds on the Soles of her Shoes'. Got that?"

Sam nodded.

"Any questions?" She didn't wait for an answer. "I need to get dressed. I'll be back downstairs before six."

God, she's a force of nature. Sam mopped his forehead.

It was Cat's nature to plan, and double check the plan. Five years in the CIA had developed these skills and it was doubtful she'd ever forget.

This year, the Syrah family had added a precious keepsake for the guests. A small program and menu had been printed for everyone. The cover was gold foil embossed with the Blue Stones Vineyard logo: a very large blue diamond entangled by grape vines.

On the back cover was a photograph of the family heirloom, a necklace made of diamonds cut from Louis XIV's French Blue. Originally purchased from a diamond dealer who had acquired it in India, Louis ordered his court jeweler to cut the one hundred and fifteen carat diamond into a heart shape, reducing it by forty-eight carats. Louis stored the small stones that fell away during the cutting in an ermine bag, then hid them where he thought no one would ever look.

Just inside the cover of the program was a short paragraph on the history of the Syrah family. Cat hoped this would address the inevitable questions about her family's last name. She'd heard it a million times. "Why is your family named after a grape?" Yuck yuck. The truth was her grandparents chose the name. They came to the United States aboard an old steamer, just after World War II. Antonio DeFabrizzio carried one small grapevine with him, the Syrah grape. Catalina (Cat's grandmother) and Antonio planned to begin their lives anew in California, but first they had to pass through Ellis Island. On the voyage across the Atlantic, the two lovers married. They chose a new name – a simple name, they thought – one that the inspectors at Ellis Island could pronounce, Syrah.

Nearly seventy years later, the Blue Stones Vineyard was among the preeminent wineries in California. The estate was nestled against the foothills of Napa Valley, facing east. Envied by the world, the rich expansive valley of twisted vines and luscious grapes competed with vintners in France, Italy, Chile, and Australia.

***

Grandma Catalina, or Nonna as she was called by her family, stood in her private suite on the second floor of the villa, watching guests arrive. Rich wine aficionados from across the globe arrived in designer clothes and exquisite jewels. Valets parked highly polished Mercedes and convertible BMWs. Limousines cruised into designated slots. Hostesses escorted guests into the villa and out onto the patio.

Nonna watched as one uninvited guest made his

way into the crowd. Dressed as a caterer in a formal white linen uniform, Nicholas Bonhomme, secret agent with the French Directorate, slipped into the mix of guests and waiters on the patio below. Glancing up, he caught Nonna's eye. She nodded.

Bonhomme joined the bartenders, just to the side of the backyard patio.

Tall and muscular, he looked like a cover model for a romance novel. Black hair tossed with mousse gave him a rakish look. His tan indicated time in the sun: golfing, playing tennis, swimming – maybe all three. Bonhomme was a magnet for women of all ages.

Sam advanced with clipboard in hand. "There are too many bartenders here. You," he said, pointing at Bonhomme, "follow me." Stopping just inside the patio door, he asked, "What's your name? You're a new hire. I want to make note of your assignment."

"Nick Edwards."

"Edwards, Edwards. Hmm, don't see your name listed," Sam said, looking up at Bonhomme.

"I believe I was the last hired," offered Bonhomme. "Perhaps my name is at the bottom of the sheet."

Sam ran his finger down the list and onto the second page, where late hires were penciled in.

"Not my handwriting, but maybe you were added by Ms. Syrah. Doesn't matter. Let's get you working. I want you at the wine bar, inside the villa, until it looks like the guests have moved through. Then go back out to the patio. Got that?"

"Yes, sir."

"Good. Now get to work."

An ultra-thin wisp of a woman in a scoop neck black dress approached the bar. "Where'd *you* come from, Mr. Gorgeous?"

Touching his hand, she asked, "You're new, aren't you, sweetie? You've never been to *our* house. Don't we rate?" A lock of copper-colored hair slipped over one eye.

"I'm new, just started today. May I serve you a drink?" The woman fit the image of a trophy wife: too much money, too much makeup, too little purpose.

"I'd like something that'll warm me to my toes. There's a little chill in the air, don't you think?" she asked, pulling her hair back behind an ear. "Do you have anything behind the bar that can help me out?" she purred.

"I have just the thing, a splash of B&B, straight up."

"Sure," she smiled, "straight up is perfect." Taking the drink from Bonhomme, she wrapped her fingers over his, locking his hand around the glass and beneath her palm.

Bonhomme heard the quaint tinkle of a delicate porcelain bell, signaling guests to take their seats. The trophy wife let go, smiling.

"See you later, gorgeous."

Bonhomme clenched his teeth.

Chapter 2
Blue Stones Villa
Napa Valley, California

The room was a sea of movement. Guests searched for assigned tables; bartenders poured Riesling into the elegant stemware; waiters lined the far wall, ready with the chilled cucumber soup.

In the midst of the churning activity, Bonhomme scanned the room. It looked like a good chance to slip out. Mumbling something to the nearest waiter, he exited down the hall.

"Not so fast," Sam said, catching Bonhomme by the sleeve as he exited down the hall. "Listen, if you think you're off to take a leak, it couldn't be a worse time. New hires," he groused. "Suck it up and get back in there!"

Merde!

Twenty-five waiters began a well-choreographed routine. They served a dollop of thick creamy soup in the center of large white bowls, followed by delicate *petite farcis*, and then a small goblet of rosemary sorbet to cleanse the palate.

With each course came a fresh glass of wine, the one most suitable for food and palate. Bonhomme moved from table to table, quietly pouring a deep red Syrah, chosen by Luciano, known to all as Luc, to complement the next course.

Cat watched Bonhomme as he approached their table. Leaning over, she whispered to her father, "Who's the new waiter?"

"Don't know. Must be one of the extras hired for tonight. You'll need to ask Sam if you want the guy's name. You interested?"

"Dad!" She whispered, shaking her head.

The entrée, a crown roast of lamb, was carved at each table. Waiters brandished sharp knives, slicing through the meat like butter, placing three small chops on each plate. A side dish of fingerling potatoes drizzled with olive oil and roasted rosemary was added, along with a small bowl containing slices of poached pear sprinkled with balsamic vinaigrette.

The women groaned, gripping their midriffs and gasping in chorus, "I can't possibly eat it all!" Husbands responded in unison with words of encouragement, "Give it a try, honey." Everyone set to work on their respective servings, planning to leave only decorative parsley and lamb bones on their gold-rimmed Lennox plates.

While the guests lingered over a salad of lightly tossed greens, the waiters caramelized the crème brûlé.

Servers cleared dishes. The well-scripted performance was nearly complete, when Bonhomme finally saw his moment.

Bonhomme glanced around for Sam. He was nowhere in sight. Slipping down the dimly lit hall, Bonhomme entered the nearest bathroom. He unsnapped his uniform, stuffed it into a towel bin, and covered it up. He'd transitioned from waiter to jewel thief.

***

Cat turned to her father. "Excuse me for a moment, Dad, but I need to check on something."

"Catalina, we're about to begin a round of introductions and toasts! You can't leave now. We'll be addressing the guests in a few minutes."

"But Dad, I'm worried …."

"Everything is fine, dear. Sam is taking care of things. That's why we pay him. The microphone is on. We need to get started."

As Cat walked to the podium, she scanned the patio. Where was he? First, he was everywhere… now nowhere. *I don't like this.*

Wearing black slacks and a tight-fitting crew neck sweater, Bonhomme stepped out of the bathroom and moved toward the Pinkerton guard at the end of the hall.

"Gotta cigarette?" Bonhomme asked casually. "I hate these fundraising events, can't even enjoy a good smoke."

Chuckling, the guard replied, "I know what you mean, but smoking is not …."

Bonhomme's hand came down hard on the side of the man's neck. The unsuspecting guard slumped over. Nicholas propped him up in a nearby chair. The guard looked a little like a Duane Hanson sculpture, just not as waxy.

Bonhomme moved up the side stairs, waited a moment, and slipped into the sitting room. Breathing softly, he listened for anyone who might have followed. No one came.

Back in the hall, he tiptoed toward Luc's study. The Directorate's floor plan was accurate. The study was four doors down the hall and just beyond the sitting room.

He was there in seconds.

Bonhomme scanned the room. Luc's mahogany desk was hard to miss. Directorate files indicated a small safe in the floor, right where Luc would normally place his feet.

Twilight left the shade-drawn room dark. Retrieving a flashlight from the small tool kit in his hip pocket, Bonhomme pulled the armchair out from behind the desk and crawled under. Flashlight on, he pulled the tiny Oriental rug back, revealing the old safe. He had the combination. Nonna had helped with that, too. He worked the dial, listening for the telltale clicks as he twisted to the right, to the left, and back to the right. Holding his breath, Bonhomme opened the safe. And, there it was ... Louis XIV's ermine bag. He untied the strings and poured the necklace into his hand. The liquid blue diamonds sparkled, even in the dimmest of light.

No time to admire. There were two other bags in the safe. Perhaps he should look in them, too. He must be certain he had the right necklace. There would be no coming back.

Voices came from down the hall. *Damn, they must have come up the central staircase.* The guards were making their rounds, opening each door and briefly inspecting the rooms. He closed the safe and hunched under the desk just before the overhead light went on.

From his hiding place, Bonhomme listened as feet moved about the room. The guard hummed to himself, turned around, switched off the lights, and exited.

Wiping cold sweat from his forehead, Bonhomme exhaled. Reopening the safe, he explored the other bags. None contained anything comparable to the necklace in the ermine bag.

A sharp click and the safe was secured. He slipped the bag into his pocket and moved to the study door. Opening it a crack, he listened. A conversation came from down the hall. The men were attempting a conversation with the Pinkerton guard, teasing him from the second floor. Suspecting he was just napping, they moved off, laughing.

A bedroom door opened. Through a tiny slit, Bonhomme watched as Nonna exited her room wearing a silver chiffon evening gown. She asked the guards to help her down the central staircase, where she would join the party for dessert and to watch Cat dance. *The perfect diversion*, thought Bonhomme. Nonna chatted as the men escorted her downstairs.

He inched his way back down the hall, then down the stairs and past the unconscious guard. Bonhomme slipped into the restroom where he planned to switch back into his uniform, but someone was in the private stall.

Merde! Just stand at the sink and wash your hands.

Music played in the living room. It sounded like Paul Simon. The man in the stall wasn't about to miss anything. Quickly zipping his pants, he scurried out without stopping to wash.

Bonhomme returned to the dining room, once again in his uniform, with the necklace tucked into his pocket.

On his way to the front door, he gathered up a half-empty case of wine and made his way to the exit. He looked around the room one more time, hoping Sam was nowhere near, and turned to leave the room. Nearly colliding with Cat, he locked eyes with her, and moved on.

"What the hell are you up to?" Sam whispered from behind. "We don't clean up until all the guests have left. You've been wrong-footed all night. Now get back over to the patio bar and don't leave until I tell you."

The music of Paul Simon's 'Diamonds on the Soles of Her Shoes' filled the house. With a little flourish, Cat and her partner began to dance. She looked deliciously seductive. Her shoes glittered with flecks of silver and she wore a short spaghetti-strap dress the color of Burgundy wine. The room quieted to whispers, as she danced the East Coast Swing. The guests were captivated.

Her eyes glistened, her movements fluid as water – or perhaps wine. She swayed, following her partner's lead. All but one member of the audience was mesmerized.

"Hey, sweetie pie, you're drooling," the drunken trophy wife whispered in Bonhomme's ear.

He stiffened.

Cat moved toward them. Silver shoes glistening, she swirled across the floor. Pausing a second, she took a handful of glitter from the sideboard and began dusting the guests, liberally sprinkling dear Nonna. She smiled. Cameras clicked.

Bonhomme recalled the Directorate reports. Cat, Nonna's namesake, was once a CIA agent but she gave it up to study art history.

How could she abandon the CIA for a reclusive academic life? He shook his head and imagined her ... a scholar wandering the dark recesses of libraries and museums researching obscure paintings and boring academic treatises. Cat was far too beautiful for such a life. She was danger laced with intrigue.

The music ended. A moment of silence followed, then robust applause. Bonhomme stepped around the trophy wife, now collapsed in a chair, legs sprawled out.

He made his way to the patio and slipped through the wrought iron gate and onto the dark path behind the villa. Finally reaching his car, parked just behind the white oak, he slid in, inadvertently scattering sliver glitter on the floor and the gearshift. The motor came to life with a soft roar.

Bonhomme exited the estate, lights on low, heading down the back roads toward San Francisco International Airport. He patted his pocket once again. The French Blues were on their way home.

Chapter 3
The Left Bank
Paris, France

Gul Mazeer balled up the front page of *Le Figaro* and tossed it into the corner of his apartment. Food cartons, newspapers, and rubbish littered the floor. Without a plan or a team, he could do nothing. He festered.

Then a smile crossed his lips, remembering the glory years of terrorism and the September 11th attack on America. He idolized the charismatic leader Osama bin Laden and he worshiped his brotherhood, al Qaeda, 'the base'. More than a decade ago, he had volunteered for an Afghan training camp. It was there that he learned military skills and the systematic techniques of terrorism. He proved himself a devoted follower of bin Laden – the terrorist leader that SEAL Team Six had killed in 2011– leaving al Qaeda headless and terrorist cells without direction.

Mazeer thought of his family, those who paid the

ultimate price for his radicalism. His mother's dead eyes never left him. Unable to drive the sight away, never wanting to drive it away, he swore vengeance. Who were these killers that had destroyed his family? Western, yes, but American? It was never known. It didn't matter. He fed on hatred.

Mazeer laughed. He was a rogue terrorist now. He could make his own plans. It was time to prove himself, and rise to the top of a new al Qaeda.

Chapter 4
Berkeley, California

The phone rang from across the room. The clock registered 3 a.m.

"Why didn't I turn that damned thing off?" Catalina mumbled, stumbling across the room. She picked it up on the third stanza of Beethoven's Fourth.

"Cat, we need to talk." It was Tadeo, from the CIA.

"Not at this hour we don't," she said, reaching for the *off* button.

"Hold on. Hold on. I know it's late, early, whatever, but you'll want to hear what I have to say."

"If you're trying to draw me back into the CIA, you can forget it. I'm done with that chapter in my life. Remember? I'm not coming back."

"Catalina, we need you. So does your family."

A chill ran up her spine. "What's this about my family?"

"Homeland Security has elevated the alert to the highest classification – the old Code Red. Terrorist cells are in constant chatter. We think an attack is imminent. The team wants you at the Pentagon as soon as you can get here. Tomorrow."

"Gee, thanks for the advance notice," she said mockingly. "And let's go back to my family. What's that all about? Just a ploy to get me there? My skills are rusty, Tad. I've been a grad student at Berkeley for the past five years. Remember?"

"You're still the best jewelry thief we've ever had."

"Family, Tad, family. I need an answer."

"Cat, talk to your father and then call me back."

"Now wait a minute! What in hell is going on? You don't call me at three in the morning and tell me to talk to my father! What's this all about?"

"Just talk to him, all right? I'd rather he told you."

"CIA agents are all alike... classified papers, Code Red, assassination watch, blah, blah, blah. Okay. Okay. I'm driving up to the house this afternoon, and there damn well better be a good reason for pulling my family into this! And Tadeo, don't ever call me at 3 a.m. again!"

The Third Knife

Book Club Discussion Questions

1. Is this book really about a knife, or does the dagger serve as a metaphor?

2. What's the importance of the Resistance flag? What does it symbolize?

3. What would you do if the United States were invaded and occupied?

4. How do Catalina and her family respond to the German invasion? Would you have done the same not knowing what the future would bring?

5. Who were the *Maquis*? Why did the Resistance movement focus on the large cities, and the *Maquis* in the countryside?

6. What is the significance of the eagle-owl, beyond the dual call? Were you surprised that the same bird could make such opposing calls? Did you know that the bird is also mentioned in *All the Light We Cannot See*?

7. Was there a good possibility France could have fractured politically after the war? Why/why not?

8. What was the meaning behind the WWI poem "Flanders Fields"? Why did the author apply it to the Second World War? How did it influence Charlotte/Catalina?

9. Who were your favorite characters? Why were you attracted to them?

10. Did you enjoy *The Third Knife?* What did it reveal to you about war, heroes, nationalism?

If you enjoyed *The Third Knife*, you might also enjoy *Return of the French Blue,* the second novel in the *Catalina & Bonhomme* series. [This is not a spoiler but a teaser: the second novel takes place in contemporary times. The new characters are the off-spring of Catalina and Edouard (Charlotte and Rémi). Nicholas Bonhomme is the son of Edouard, and Cat is the granddaughter of Catalina "Nonna" Settevendemie.]

www.ingramcontent.com/pod-product-compliance
Lightning Source LLC
LaVergne TN
LVHW051541080426
835510LV00020B/2810